Betty Crocker's
NEW
BOYS AND GIRLS
COOKBOOK

Betty Crocker's
NEW
BOYS
AND
GIRLS
COOKBOOK

PRENTICE HALL

New York ● London ◆ Toronto

Sydney ★ Tokyo ▲ Singapore

PRENTICE HALL GENERAL REFERENCE
15 Columbus Circle
New York, NY 10023

Published simultaneously in Canada by Prentice Hall Canada Inc.

PRENTICE HALL and colophons are registered trademarks of Simon & Schuster, Inc.

BETTY CROCKER is a registered trademark of General Mills, Inc.

Library of Congress Cataloging-in-Publication Data

Crocker, Betty.
    [New boys and girls cookbook]
    Betty Crocker's new boys and girls cookbook.
        p.   cm.
    Summary: Features more than 140 easy-to-prepare recipes developed for the young cook.
    ISBN 0-13-083262-6:
    1. Cookery—Juvenile literature.   [1. Cookery.] I. Title.
TX652.5.C7   1990
641.5'123—dc20   89-26485
                                              CIP
                                              AC

Manufactured in the United States of America

10 9 8 7 6 5 4

First Edition

PRENTICE HALL
Senior Vice-President and Publisher: *Nina Hoffman*
Senior Editor: *Rebecca W. Atwater*
Editorial Assistant: *Rachel A. Simon*
Assistant Art Director: *Patricia Fabricant*
Designers: *Frederick J. Latasa, Angela G. Carlino*
Illustrator: *Mary Lynn Blasutta*
Prop Stylist: *IDESIGN*
Production Editor: *Kimberly A. Ebert*
Senior Production Manager: *Susan Joseph*

GENERAL MILLS, INC.
Editor: *Maureen Powers Fischer*
Recipe Development Editor: *Diana Gulden*
Recipe Copy Editor: *Deb Hance*
Administrative Assistant: *Pam Jones*
Food Stylists: *Cindy Lund, Mary Sethre*
Photographer: *Nanci E. Doonan*
Photography Assistant: *Chuck Carver*
Director, Betty Crocker Food and Publications Center: *Marcia Copeland*
Assistant Manager Publications: *Lois Tlusty*
Drawing featured in photograph on pages 32–33 by *Jennifer Dolland.*

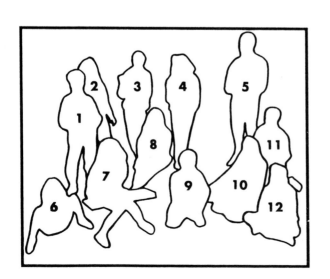

Our Panel of Kitchen Testers, preceeding page: (1) Scott Ferguson (2) Jenna Farni (3) Ryan Setterholm (4) Robin Trautman (5) Jennifer Dolland (6) Katie Barber (7) Malia Kinsman (8) Jenny Reese (9) Jeremy Jones (10) Edith Cizio (11) Nate Swenson (12) Hilary Burnham

Contents

Introduction

We made this cookbook just for you! These recipes were developed for kids—tested and approved by kids, too—so they're fun, easy and best of all, *really* delicious. You will want to try everything, from Oh-So-Chocolate Brownies and Banana-Orange Frost to Fiesta Chili and Yogurt Sundaes . . . with fifteen toppings to choose from! You can make your own hot breakfast, dinner for your whole family, even plan a special party.

All your favorites—like fresh pizza, juicy hamburgers and zesty nachos with cheese—are here. We've included lots of other delicious foods that just might become favorites, too. How about Big Puffy Pancake: a pancake that you bake in a skillet in the oven, so it puffs up big? Or a heart-shaped cake for Valentine's Day or Mother's Day?

Don't forget to read carefully any important safety tips and hints you will find along with the recipes. If you have any questions, ask an adult to help you. And you can show appreciation for your family by cooking clean, safe and smart.

Check out the special menus on page 136 to help you plan special events: parties, breakfast in bed, a picnic, even a Halloween event. Feel free to be creative with your recipes and make them your own. Our panel of home testers and tasters (meet them on page iv) sometimes changed recipes to suit their taste, and they pass on their suggestions to you in these pages. Of course, you will come up with suggestions of your own, because you're in charge! We hope you enjoy cooking with us, today and for many years to come.

THE BETTY CROCKER EDITORS

Cook's Corner

- Before you use a sharp knife, can opener, blender, mixer or microwave oven, be sure someone older is in the kitchen to help you and to answer questions.

- Turn off the blender or mixer before you scrape the sides of the container or bowl. This way you can be sure the scraper won't get caught in the blades.

- Turn off the mixer and be sure it's unplugged whenever you put the beaters in or take them out.

- Never disconnect an appliance by pulling on the cord. Pull out the plug instead.

- Ask someone older to drain foods cooked in lots of hot water (like macaroni). Pans full of water are heavy, and if it isn't done just right, the steam could burn you.

- Turn the handles of saucepans on the range away from you so they won't catch on anything and tip over.

- Always dry your hands after you wash them to avoid slippery fingers and shocks from electrical outlets.

- Wipe up spills right away to avoid slippery floors.

- Avoid burns by using thick, dry potholders, not thin or wet ones. Always use potholders when handling hot items, or when putting an item in or removing it from the oven.

- Always turn the sharp edge of a knife or vegetable parer away from you and your hand when you chop or pare foods.

- When slicing or chopping ingredients, be sure to use a cutting board.

1

COOK'S CHECKLIST

- Check with the adults in your family for a convenient time to make the recipe.

- Wash your hands and wear an apron. You might want to tie back your hair if it's long so it won't get in the way.

- Read the recipe all the way through before starting to cook.

- Set out a tray and all ingredients listed in the top of the recipe. Put them on the tray. Set out all the utensils. When the tray is empty, you'll know you haven't left out any ingredients.

- Clean up as you go along. As you finish using a utensil, put it in warm soapy water to soak. Oops! Don't put the knives in! Wash them separately, and be careful of the sharp blades.

- Wash and dry all the utensils you have used, and put them away. Wash the counters, and leave the kitchen neat and clean.

- Check the range, oven and any other appliances to be sure you have turned them off. Put away any appliances you have used.

- Now, enjoy your creation!

GLOSSARY OF COOKING TERMS

BEAT. Make smooth with a vigorous stirring motion using a spoon, wire whisk or eggbeater.

BOIL. Heat liquid until bubbles keep rising and breaking on the surface.

CORE. Cut out stem end and remove the seeds.

DRAIN. Pour off liquid or let it run off through the holes in a strainer or colander, as when draining cooked pasta.

Or remove pieces of food from a fat or liquid and set them on paper towels to soak up excess moisture.

GREASE. Spread the bottoms and sides of a pan with shortening.

KNEAD. Curve your fingers and fold dough toward you, then push it away with the heels of your hands, using a quick rocking motion.

MIX. Combine to distribute ingredients evenly using an electric mixer, blender or spoon.

PARE. Cut off the skin.

SIMMER. Heat liquid until just below the boiling point; bubbles form slowly and collapse below the surface.

STAND. After taking the food out of the oven, let it just sit for the amount of time called for in the recipe.

WHIP. Beat rapidly to make light and fluffy, using an electric mixer or eggbeater.

USING APPLIANCES

THE OVEN

- If the racks need to be adjusted higher or lower, be sure to arrange them before you turn on the oven.

- Allow plenty of air space around foods you're baking—no containers should touch.

- Arrange foods on oven racks so that one isn't placed directly over another.

- Use a tight-fitting lid or aluminum foil when the recipe calls for covering. Uncover cooked foods away from you, and keep your face away from the steam.

- Close the oven door quickly when you have finished looking in, so heat won't be lost.

THE RANGE OR STOVE TOP

- Put large pans on large burners, small pans on small burners. Turn the handles of pots and pans so they don't stick out over the edge of the range, where they might accidentally be bumped, and make sure they're not over another burner either.

THE MICROWAVE OVEN

- Read the instruction booklet to find out the kinds of foods your oven cooks best and the correct cooking times.

- Most foods should be covered to prevent spattering.

- Allow a few minutes standing time after cooking foods, since they continue to cook after you take them out of the oven.

- Be careful not to burn yourself. Even though microwaves go right through containers without heating them, the heat of the food can make the containers hot.

TABLE TALK

A nice-looking table makes mealtime more fun! Here are some basics to make your tabletop top-notch.

- Place the dinner plate about one inch from the edge of the table.

- Place the knife to the right of the plate. The blade should face toward the plate.

- Place the spoon to the right of the knife.

- The fork goes to the left of the plate with the tines facing up.

- The beverage glass should be placed directly above the point of the knife. If you plan to use a cup and saucer, place them to the right of the spoon.

- If you plan to use a salad plate, it should be placed to the left of the fork.

- Napkins should be placed to the left of the fork with the open corner toward you. This makes it easy to open. Try using napkin rings with either cloth or paper napkins to make the table look really special!

KITCHEN MATH

 = ½ gallon

3 teaspoons = 1 tablespoon

 = 1 quart

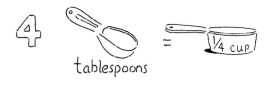
4 tablespoons = ¼ cup

 = 1 Pint

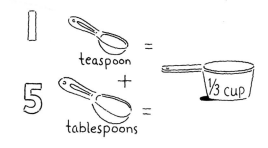
1 teaspoon + 5 tablespoons = ⅓ cup

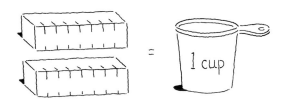 = 1 cup

8 tablespoons = ½ cup

 = ½ cup

= ¼ cup

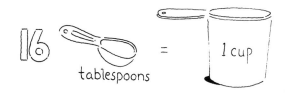
16 tablespoons = 1 cup

UTENSILS YOU SHOULD HAVE

FOR PREPARATION

Apple Corer

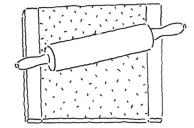
Covered rolling pin and board

Wire whisk

Kitchen scissors

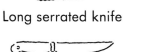
Long serrated knife

Potato masher

Juicer

Timer

Can opener

Sharp knife

Vegetable parer

Ice-cream scoop

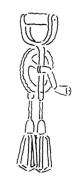
Colander

Eggbeater

Vegetable brush

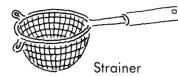
Strainer

Custard cups
(6- and 10-ounce)

Pastry brush

Biscuit cutter

Cookie cutter

Mixing bowls (set of 3)

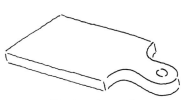
Cutting board

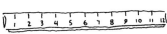
Ruler

Rubber scraper

FOR MEASURING

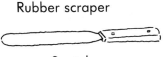
Spatula

Liquid measuring cup
(1-cup)

Measuring spoons
(¼, ½, 1-teaspoon,
1-tablespoon)

Dry measuring cups
(1, ½, ⅓, ¼-cup)

FOR TOP-OF-RANGE COOKING

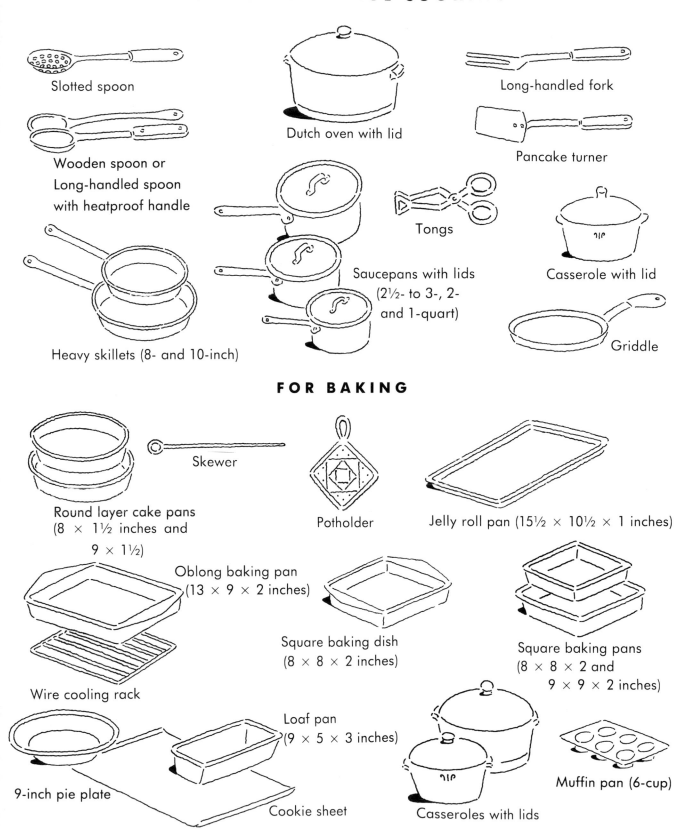

Slotted spoon

Dutch oven with lid

Long-handled fork

Wooden spoon or
Long-handled spoon
with heatproof handle

Pancake turner

Tongs

Saucepans with lids
(2½- to 3-, 2-
and 1-quart)

Casserole with lid

Heavy skillets (8- and 10-inch)

Griddle

FOR BAKING

Skewer

Potholder

Jelly roll pan (15½ × 10½ × 1 inches)

Round layer cake pans
(8 × 1½ inches and
9 × 1½)

Oblong baking pan
(13 × 9 × 2 inches)

Square baking dish
(8 × 8 × 2 inches)

Square baking pans
(8 × 8 × 2 and
9 × 9 × 2 inches)

Wire cooling rack

Loaf pan
(9 × 5 × 3 inches)

9-inch pie plate

Cookie sheet

Casseroles with lids

Muffin pan (6-cup)

7

THE RIGHT MEASURE

ALL-PURPOSE FLOUR. Spoon flour lightly into dry measuring cup. Level with spatula. Variety baking mix and granulated and powdered sugar are measured the same way.

CHOPPED NUTS. Pack lightly into dry measuring cup. Also measure shredded cheese, soft bread crumbs and shredded coconut this way.

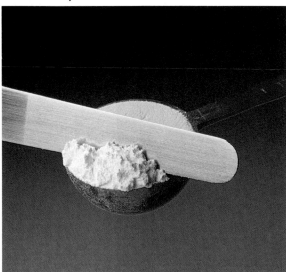

BAKING POWDER. Dip and fill measuring spoon. Level with spatula. Baking soda, cream of tartar and spices are measured in the same way. Liquids, like vanilla, can also be measured in measuring spoons.

BROWN SUGAR. Pack firmly into dry measuring cup. Level with spatula.

SHORTENING. Pack firmly into dry measuring cup. Level with spatula and remove with rubber scraper.

MOLASSES AND CORN SYRUP. Pour into liquid measuring cup. Remove with rubber scraper.

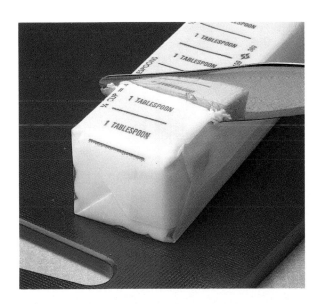

MARGARINE OR BUTTER. Cut using measurement marks on the wrapper as a guide.

MILK AND OTHER LIQUIDS. Set liquid measuring cup on counter. Pour in the liquid. Bend down to check the correct amount at eye level.

Super Snacks and Drinks

1

Rainbow Float (page 14), Banana-Orange Frost (page 12), Very Strawberry Soda (page 13), Cheesy Pretzels (page 28)

*B*anana-Orange Frost

1 serving

INGREDIENTS	UTENSILS
▪ Milk	▪ Blender
▪ Orange juice	▪ Liquid measuring cup
▪ Orange sherbet	▪ Ice-cream scoop
▪ Banana	▪ Table knife
	▪ Cutting board
	▪ Tall glass

Put into blender container

> ¼ cup milk
> ¼ cup orange juice
> 1 large scoop orange sherbet
> (about ½ cup)
> 1 small banana, cut into pieces

Cover and blend on high speed 10 seconds. Pour into a tall glass.

Top with

> 1 small scoop orange sherbet
> (about ¼ cup)

Serve right away.

*C*hocolate Milk Shake

2 servings

INGREDIENTS	UTENSILS
▪ Milk	▪ Blender
▪ Chocolate-flavored syrup	▪ Liquid measuring cup
▪ Vanilla ice cream	▪ Ice-cream scoop
	▪ Tall glasses

Put in blender container

> ¾ cup milk
> ¼ cup chocolate-flavored syrup
> 3 large scoops vanilla ice cream
> (about 1½ cups)

Cover and blend on low speed about 10 seconds or until smooth.

Pour into 2 tall glasses. Serve right away.

CHOCOLATE–PEANUT BUTTER MILK SHAKE: Add 2 tablespoons peanut butter to the milk, chocolate-flavored syrup and ice cream before blending.

CHOCOLATE-MINT MILK SHAKE: Add ½ teaspoon peppermint extract to the milk, chocolate-flavored syrup and ice cream before blending.

This Chocolate Milk Shake was a hit! **Jenny** *described this frosty drink as "the richest, creamiest Chocolate Milk Shake!" You can make this milk shake with any flavor ice cream.*

*V*ery Strawberry Soda

1 soda

INGREDIENTS

- Strawberry ice-cream topping
- Pineapple ice-cream topping
- Vanilla ice cream
- Strawberry carbonated beverage

UTENSILS

- Tall glass
- Measuring spoons
- Ice-cream scoop
- Long-handled spoon
- Liquid measuring cup

Mix in a tall glass

> 2 tablespoons strawberry ice-cream topping
> 2 tablespoons pineapple ice-cream topping
> 1 small scoop vanilla ice cream (about ¼ cup)

Stir in

> ¼ cup chilled strawberry carbonated beverage

Add

> 3 medium scoops vanilla ice cream (about 1 cup)

Fill glass with

> chilled strawberry carbonated beverage

Serve right away.

*P*ineapple Fizz

2 servings

INGREDIENTS

- Pineapple juice
- Pineapple sherbet
- Sparkling water

UTENSILS

- Blender
- Liquid measuring cup
- Ice-cream scoop
- Tall glasses

Put in blender container

> 1½ cups pineapple juice
> 2 large scoops pineapple sherbet (about 1 cup)
> ½ cup sparkling water

Cover and blend on low speed 10 seconds or until the mixture is smooth.

Pour into 2 tall glasses. Serve right away.

Nate *loved Pineapple Fizz! Not only did he find this cool drink "simple and refreshing," but he thought it was "fast, easy and fun."*

ainbow Float

1 float

INGREDIENTS

- Red fruit punch drink or fruit juice
- Lemon sherbet
- Lemon-lime carbonated beverage or sparkling water

UTENSILS

- Tall glass
- Ice-cream scoop

Fill a tall glass halfway with

> red fruit punch drink or fruit juice

Scoop into the glass

> 2 medium scoops lemon sherbet (about ⅔ cup)

Fill the glass with

> lemon-lime carbonated beverage or sparkling water

Serve right away.

*H*ot Chocolate

5 servings

INGREDIENTS

- Milk
- Chocolate-flavored syrup

UTENSILS

- 2-quart saucepan
- Liquid measuring cup
- Large spoon
- Beverage mugs
- Soup ladle

Pour into saucepan

> 3 cups milk

Heat over medium heat until hot but not boiling.

Stir in until well blended

> ⅓ to ½ cup chocolate-flavored syrup

Put the hot chocolate into mugs with a soup ladle.

HINT: *Serve with whipped cream, marshmallows or sticks of cinnamon candy if you like.*

TO MICROWAVE: Pour milk into 4-cup microwavable measure. Microwave uncovered on high (100%) 5 to 6 minutes or until hot. Stir in chocolate-flavored syrup until well blended. Put hot chocolate into mugs with a soup ladle.

*P*ickle Snack Slices

1 snack

INGREDIENTS

- Large dill or sweet pickle
- Soft cream cheese
- Ham

UTENSILS

- Paper towel
- Ruler
- Measuring spoons
- Table knife
- Sharp knife
- Cutting board

Pat dry with a paper towel

> 1 large dill or sweet pickle, about 4 inches long

Spread 1 tablespoon soft cream cheese on

> 1 slice fully cooked smoked ham, about 4 × 4 inches

Place pickle on ham. Wrap around the pickle.

Cut the wrapped pickle into ½-inch slices.

Pickle Snack Slices proved to be a fun snack—not only to make, but to eat, too! **Jenny** *declared, "I thought it looked just like a kids' appetizer."*

*A*pple-Cheese Snack

1 snack

INGREDIENTS

- Apple
- Cheddar, American or Swiss cheese

UTENSILS

- Apple corer
- Sharp knife
- Cutting board
- Small plate

Wash and core

> 1 medium apple

Cut into fourths, then cut each fourth into 4 or 5 slices. Arrange in circle on plate.

Cut into wedges

> Small chunk of Cheddar, American or Swiss cheese

Put cheese wedges in the center of the plate.

Serve right away.

HINT: *To keep apple slices from turning brown, dip in lemon juice.*

*F*ruit in a Cone

1 cone

INGREDIENTS

- Large ice-cream cone
- Fruit
- Honey
- Granola

UTENSILS

- Sharp knife
- Cutting board
- Dry measuring cups
- Measuring spoons

Put in the ice-cream cone

> about ¾ cup cut-up fruit (enough to fill to rim). Choose from any of these fruits:
> strawberries
> bananas
> apples
> blueberries
> raspberries
> pears
> grapes

Drizzle with

> 1 teaspoon honey

Sprinkle with

> 1 teaspoon granola

HINT: *Make these extra fun by dipping the cones in melted chocolate before you fill them.*

Can food be "fun"? **Malia** *thinks so! That's how she described Fruit in a Cone.*

*S*trawberry Fruit Leather

1 roll

INGREDIENTS

- Strawberries
- Honey or corn syrup

UTENSILS

- Jelly roll pan, 15½ × 10½ × 1 inch
- Plastic wrap
- Blender
- Sharp knife
- Cutting board
- Dry measuring cup
- Measuring spoons
- Rubber scraper
- Potholders

Heat oven to 140°.

Line jelly roll pan with plastic wrap.

Put in blender container

> 1 cup cut-up strawberries
> 2 teaspoons honey or corn syrup

Cover and blend about 10 seconds or until the mixture is smooth. Pour strawberry mixture in the center of the jelly roll pan. Spread the mixture evenly in the pan with rubber scraper.

With the oven door slightly open, bake about 3 hours or until dry. Cool; roll in plastic wrap to store.

Hilary *liked the "fruity flavor" of Strawberry Fruit Leather. "It's a good snack."*

*F*ruit on Skewers

1 serving

INGREDIENTS **UTENSILS**

- Pineapple chunks
- Apple chunks
- Banana pieces
- Grapes

- Metal skewers
- Sharp knife
- Cutting board
- Fork

Place on skewers (ask an adult to help you)

> pineapple chunks
> apple chunks
> banana pieces
> grapes

Repeat until you have filled as many skewers as you want. Serve right away. To eat the fruit, push it off the skewer with a fork.

HINT: *Try making Fruit on Skewers with your favorite fruits!*

*E*asy Cheesy Spread

1⅓ cups spread

INGREDIENTS **UTENSILS**

- Whipped cream cheese
- Finely shredded Cheddar cheese
- Instant minced onion
- Dijon or regular mustard
- Worcestershire sauce
- Chopped nuts
- Crackers

- Medium bowl
- Dry measuring cup
- Measuring spoons
- Long-handled spoon
- Small bowl
- Plastic wrap

Mix together in medium bowl

> 1 container (8 ounces) whipped cream cheese
> 1 cup finely shredded Cheddar cheese (4 ounces)
> ½ teaspoon instant minced onion
> 1 teaspoon Dijon or regular mustard
> 1 teaspoon Worcestershire sauce

Put the cheese mixture in small bowl.

Sprinkle the cheese mixture with

> 2 tablespoons chopped nuts

Cover with plastic wrap and refrigerate about 2 hours or until cold.

Serve spread with crackers.

HINT: *Easy Cheesy Spread is also good for sandwiches.*

ippy Vegetable Dip

2 cups dip

INGREDIENTS

- Cottage cheese
- Plain yogurt or sour cream
- Ranch-style salad dressing mix
- Vegetable "dippers"

UTENSILS

- Blender
- Dry measuring cup
- Rubber scraper
- Serving bowl
- Sharp knife
- Cutting board

Put in blender container

> 1 cup cottage cheese
> 1 cup plain yogurt or sour cream
> 1 package (1 ounce) ranch-style salad dressing mix

Cover and blend on medium speed about 30 seconds or until the mixture is smooth. Stop the blender a few times to scrape mixture down from the sides. (Be sure to put the lid back on before starting blender again.)

Put dip in serving bowl. Serve dip with any of these vegetable "dippers."

> carrot sticks
> celery sticks
> cucumber slices
> small chunks of broccoli
> small chunks of cauliflower
> your favorite raw vegetable

Quick Fruit Dip

1 cup dip

INGREDIENTS

- Plain yogurt
- Brown sugar
- Fruit

UTENSILS

- Small bowl
- Dry measuring cup
- Measuring spoons
- Spoon
- Sharp knife
- Cutting board

Mix together in small bowl

> 1 cup plain yogurt
> 2 tablespoons brown sugar

Serve with any of these fruits

> apple wedges
> strawberries
> grapes
> banana slices
> pineapple chunks

Hilary *liked delicious Quick Fruit Dip! She commented, "It tastes good on a sunny day and is easy."*

*S*nickersnack

7 cups snack

INGREDIENTS

- Toasted oat cereal
- Salted peanuts
- Raisins
- Margarine or butter
- Semisweet chocolate chips

UTENSILS

- Large bowl
- Dry measuring cup
- Long-handled spoon
- 1-quart saucepan
- Fork

Mix in large bowl

> 4 cups toasted oat cereal
> 1 can (6½ ounces) salted peanuts
> 1 cup raisins

Heat in saucepan over low heat until melted (ask an adult to help you)

> ¼ cup margarine or butter

Pour the melted margarine over the cereal mixture, using fork to toss lightly until the mixture is coated.

Sprinkle over the mixture and toss again

> 1 cup semisweet chocolate chips (6 ounces)

Store in an airtight container.

*"B*eary" Good Snack Mix

6 cups snack

INGREDIENTS

- Bear-shaped graham snacks
- Honey-nut toasted oat cereal
- Honey-roasted peanuts
- Raisins

UTENSILS

- Large bowl
- Dry measuring cups
- Long-handled spoon
- Plastic bag or covered container

Mix together in large bowl

> 2 cups bear-shaped graham snacks
> 2 cups honey-nut toasted oat cereal
> 1 cup honey-roasted peanuts
> ½ cup raisins

Store in a plastic bag or covered container.

Robin had few improvements to "Beary" Good Snack Mix. Her only addition: "Maybe I'd add a little more peanuts."

"Beary" Good Snack Mix, Hot Chocolate (page 14)

$\mathcal{M}$unchy Crunchy Granola

4 cups granola

INGREDIENTS

- Margarine or butter
- Brown sugar
- Vanilla
- Dried apples, apricots or mixed fruit
- Oats
- Raisins
- Salted toasted sunflower seed
- Sesame seed

UTENSILS

- Rectangular pan, 13 × 9 × 2 inches
- Dry measuring cups
- Potholders
- Long-handled spoon
- Measuring spoons
- Scissors

Heat oven to 350°.

Heat in rectangular pan until melted (ask an adult to help you)

> ¼ cup margarine or butter

Remove pan from oven.

Stir in until well blended

> ¼ cup packed brown sugar
> 2 teaspoons vanilla

Cut into small pieces with scissors

> ½ cup dried apples, apricots or mixed fruit

In pan, stir apple pieces and

> 1½ cups oats
> 1 cup raisins
> ¼ cup salted toasted sunflower seed
> ¼ cup sesame seed

Mix well. Bake uncovered for 10 minutes.

Remove from oven and stir. Return to oven and bake 10 minutes longer. Cool.

Use granola as a topping for cereal or ice cream, or serve in bowls, pack in small plastic bags for snacks or lunch box treats.

Store any leftover granola in tightly covered container in refrigerator

TO MICROWAVE: Put margarine in 2-quart microwavable casserole or bowl.

Microwave uncovered on high (100%) 30 to 45 seconds or until margarine is melted. Stir in brown sugar and vanilla until completely blended.

Stir in remaining ingredients except raisins. Microwave uncovered on high (100%) 2 minutes; stir. Microwave 1 to 2 minutes longer or until toasted (watch carefully so mixture does not burn). Stir in raisins.

Super Simple S'Mores

24 squares

INGREDIENTS

- Shortening
- Corn syrup
- Margarine or butter
- Milk chocolate chips
- Vanilla
- Honey graham cereal
- Miniature marshmallows

UTENSILS

- Rectangular pan, 13 × 9 × 2 inches
- 2-quart saucepan
- Liquid measuring cup
- Long-handled spoon
- Measuring spoons
- Very large bowl
- Dry measuring cup
- Large spoon
- Sharp knife
- Ruler

Grease rectangular pan with shortening.

Heat to boiling in saucepan, stirring all the time

> ¾ cup corn syrup
> 3 tablespoons margarine or butter
> 1 package (11½ ounces) milk chocolate chips

Remove pan from heat.

Stir in

> 1 teaspoon vanilla

Pour into very large bowl

> 1 package (12 ounces) honey graham cereal (9 cups)

Pour chocolate mixture over cereal; toss until completely coated with chocolate.

Stir in, 1 cup at a time

> 3 cups miniature marshmallows

Press mixture evenly in pan with buttered back of large spoon.

Let stand at room temperature at least 1 hour or until firm.

Cut into 2-inch squares. Store loosely covered at room temperature no longer than 2 days.

TO MICROWAVE: Mix corn syrup, margarine and chocolate chips in 4-cup microwavable measure or 1-quart microwavable bowl.

Cover with plastic wrap. Turn 1 edge of plastic wrap back to make a little space for steam to come out.

Microwave on high (100%) 2 to 3 minutes or until boiling. Carefully remove plastic wrap; add vanilla.

Stir until chips are melted and mixture is smooth. Finish as directed above.

*C*hocolate-Popcorn Bars

24 bars

INGREDIENTS

- Semisweet chocolate chips
- Popped corn

UTENSILS

- 1-quart saucepan
- Long-handled spoon
- Large bowl
- Dry measuring cup
- Rectangular pan, 12 × 7½ × 2 inches
- Table knife

Put in saucepan

> 1 package (12 ounces) semisweet chocolate chips

Cook over low heat, stirring often, until the chocolate chips are melted and smooth.

Put in large bowl

> 8 cups popped corn

Pour the melted chocolate over popped corn. Stir well to evenly coat popped corn with chocolate.

Pour popped corn mixture into rectangular pan. Press mixture firmly into pan with back of spoon.

Refrigerate about 1 hour or until chocolate is firm. Cut into 24 bars. Refrigerate any remaining bars.

TO MICROWAVE: Pour chocolate chips into 1-quart microwavable bowl.

Cover with plastic wrap. Turn 1 edge of plastic wrap back to make a little space for steam to come out.

Microwave on medium (50%) until chips are shiny, 4 to 6 minutes. Stir until smooth. Finish as directed above.

HINT: *If bars crumble when cutting, let stand at room temperature 15 minutes or until chocolate softens a little.*

Yogurt Sundaes

1 serving

INGREDIENTS

- Plain or flavored yogurt
- Fruit Toppings
- Crunchy Toppings

UTENSILS

- Small bowl
- Dry measuring cup
- Measuring spoons

Place in small bowl

½ cup plain or flavored yogurt

Top with

1 or 2 tablespoons of ONE of the Fruit Toppings 1 tablespoon of ONE of the Crunchy Toppings

FRUIT TOPPINGS

- Sliced strawberries
- Blueberries
- Sliced bananas
- Crushed pineapple
- Fruit cocktail
- Mandarin orange segments
- Peach slices
- Raisins

CRUNCHY TOPPINGS

- Granola
- Shredded coconut
- Mini chocolate chips
- Cereal
- Peanuts
- Sunflower nuts
- Trail mix

Peanut Butter and Banana "Dog"

1 serving

INGREDIENTS

- Hot dog bun
- Peanut butter
- Banana

UTENSILS

- Sharp knife
- Measuring spoons
- Table knife

Split

1 hot dog bun

Spread bun with

1 or 2 tablespoons peanut butter

Peel and place in the bun

1 small banana

CHOCOLATE BANANA "DOG": In place of peanut butter, spread bun with 1 tablespoon chocolate-nut spread.

HINT: *Choose a straight banana. It fits better in the bun.*

*F*rozen Tropical Dream Pops

7 pops

INGREDIENTS

- Plain yogurt
- Crushed pineapple
- Frozen orange juice concentrate

UTENSILS

- Medium bowl
- Dry measuring cups
- Long-handled spoon
- 3-ounce paper or plastic cups
- Wooden sticks

Mix together in medium bowl

> 2 cups plain yogurt
> ½ cup crushed pineapple
> 1 can (6 ounces) frozen orange juice concentrate, thawed

Spoon the mixture into 7 paper cups.

Freeze about 45 minutes or until the mixture begins to thicken.

Place a wooden stick in the center of each pop. Freeze about 4 hours or until pops are solid.

Peel the paper cups from frozen pops before eating.

HINT: *You don't need wooden sticks to make these pops. Freeze without the sticks. Just peel the paper cup as you eat the pop.*

*P*ink Lemonade Pops

7 pops

INGREDIENTS

- Cranberry juice
- Frozen lemonade concentrate

UTENSILS

- Large pitcher
- Liquid measuring cup
- Long-handled spoon
- 3-ounce paper or plastic cups
- Wooden sticks

Pour into large pitcher and mix together

> 1 cup cranberry juice
> ½ cup water
> 1 can (6 ounces) frozen lemonade concentrate, thawed

Pour the mixture into 7 paper cups.

Freeze about 1 hour or until the mixture is thick and slushy.

Place a wooden stick in the center of each pop. Freeze about 7 hours longer or until pops are solid.

Peel the paper cups from frozen pops before eating.

These Pink Lemonade Pops received a top-notch rating! "These pops are refreshing to the mouth," says **Malia**.

*F*rozen "Yogonanas"

4 servings

INGREDIENTS

- Graham cereal
- Bananas
- Yogurt

UTENSILS

- Waxed paper
- Dinner plate
- Plastic bag
- Dry measuring cups
- Rolling pin
- Table knife
- Cutting board
- Wooden sticks
- Shallow bowl

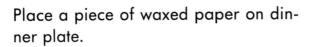

Place a piece of waxed paper on dinner plate.

Put in plastic bag and crush with rolling pin

1 cup graham cereal

Peel and cut in half crosswise

2 large bananas

Carefully insert a wooden stick into the cut end of each banana half.

Put in shallow bowl

½ cup plain or flavored yogurt

Roll bananas in the yogurt. Sprinkle some of the crushed cereal over each yogurt-covered banana.

Place bananas on the waxed paper-lined dinner plate.

Freeze about 2 hours or until "yogonanas" are hard.

*C*heesy Pretzels

16 pretzels

INGREDIENTS

- Shortening
- Flour
- Milk
- Shredded Cheddar cheese
- Margarine or butter
- Baking powder
- Sugar
- Salt
- Egg
- Coarse salt

UTENSILS

- Cookie sheet
- Breadboard and pastry cloth
- Rolling pin and cloth cover
- Medium bowl
- Dry measuring cups
- Liquid measuring cup
- Measuring spoons
- Fork
- Table knife
- Ruler
- Small bowl
- Pastry brush
- Potholders
- Pancake turner
- Wire cooling rack

Heat oven to 400°.

Grease cookie sheet with shortening.

Cover breadboard with pastry cloth, tucking ends underneath. Cover rolling pin with cloth cover.

Sprinkle the covered board and rolling pin lightly with the flour and rub it in until it disappears.

Mix together in medium bowl with fork

> 1½ cups all-purpose flour
> ⅔ cup milk
> ½ cup shredded Cheddar cheese
> 2 tablespoons margarine or butter
> 2 teaspoons baking powder
> 1 teaspoon sugar
> ½ teaspoon salt

Gently smooth the dough into a ball on the covered board. Knead 10 times.

Divide the dough in half. Cover 1 half.

Roll half of dough into a 12 × 8-inch rectangle. Mark and cut the rectangle lengthwise into eight 1-inch strips.

Make each strip narrower by folding it in half lengthwise. Pinch edges to seal.

Twist each strip into a pretzel shape and place, pinched side down, on the cookie sheet.

 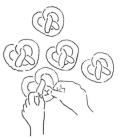

Beat in small bowl with fork

> 1 egg

Brush the pretzels with the beaten egg, then sprinkle lightly with

> coarse salt

Bake 20 to 25 minutes or until golden brown. Remove with pancake turner to wire rack. Repeat with remaining half of the dough.

*N*ifty Nachos

5 servings

INGREDIENTS

- Round tortilla chips
- Chopped mild green chilies
- Shredded Monterey Jack or Cheddar cheese

UTENSILS

- Cookie sheet
- Aluminum foil
- Can opener
- Strainer
- Dry measuring cups
- Potholders

Heat oven to 400°.

Line cookie sheet with aluminum foil.

Put on the cookie sheet

> 30 round tortilla chips

Divide evenly over the tortilla chips

> ¼ cup chopped mild green chilies, drained

Sprinkle on top of the chilies and chips

> 1¼ cups shredded Monterey Jack or Cheddar cheese (5 ounces)

Bake about 4 minutes or until the cheese is melted.

Carefully remove the cookie sheet from the oven. Serve with salsa if you like.

NACHOS WITH SALSA: Spoon mild salsa on the tortilla chips in place of the chopped green chilies.

TO MICROWAVE 1 SERVING: Arrange 6 tortilla chips in a circle on microwavable dinner plate. Spoon a small amount of salsa on each chip. Microwave uncovered on high (100%) 20 to 30 seconds or until the cheese is melted.

*"I think I've died and gone to heaven!" That's exactly how **Robin** described Nifty Nachos. An extra bonus, says Robin, "We didn't have to clean the cookie sheet."*

Nachos with Salsa

Good Morning Eye Openers

2

Wonderful Waffles (page 38)

Shake-'em-up Scrambled Eggs

4 servings

INGREDIENTS	UTENSILS
▪ Tomato	▪ Sharp knife
▪ Eggs	▪ Cutting board
▪ Shredded Cheddar cheese	▪ 1-quart jar with lid
▪ Salt	▪ Dry measuring cup
▪ Pepper	▪ Measuring spoons
▪ Margarine or butter	▪ 10-inch skillet
	▪ Pancake turner

Wash and chop into small pieces

> 1 medium tomato

Put tomato pieces in jar.

Add

> 4 eggs
> ½ cup shredded Cheddar cheese
> (2 ounces)
> ¼ teaspoon salt
> dash of pepper

Cover the jar tightly and shake well.

Heat until melted in skillet over medium heat (ask an adult to help you)

> 1 tablespoon margarine or butter

Tilt skillet so inside of skillet is coated with the melted margarine.

Pour the egg mixture into the hot skillet and cook over medium heat without stirring.

Turn gently with pancake turner when the eggs on the bottom start to get firm.

Cook 5 to 8 minutes or until the eggs are slightly firm but not runny.

TO MICROWAVE: Use ingredients listed above except do not use margarine. Beat eggs, salt and pepper with fork in 1-quart microwavable casserole or bowl. Stir in chopped tomato and the cheese. Cover casserole with lid or plastic wrap. If using plastic wrap, turn back 1 edge to make a little space for steam to come out.

Microwave on high (100%) 1 minute. Very carefully remove the lid; stir eggs. Stir eggs 3 times (cover casserole, microwave on high 1 minute and stir). (Dish may be hot at the end of cooking, so use potholders.) Eggs should be slightly firm but not runny.

HINT: *1 small stalk celery, washed and chopped, or 1 small green bell pepper, washed and chopped, can be used in place of the tomato. Add ¼ cup milk.*

$\mathcal{J}$elly Omelet

1 serving

INGREDIENTS

- Eggs
- Salt
- Margarine or butter
- Jelly or jam

UTENSILS

- Small bowl
- Fork
- 8-inch skillet or omelet pan
- Measuring spoons
- Pancake turner

Beat in small bowl with fork

> 2 eggs
> dash of salt

Heat in skillet or omelet pan over medium-high heat (ask an adult to help you)

> 1 tablespoon margarine or butter

Tilt skillet so the inside of skillet is coated with the melted margarine. Pour the eggs into the skillet.

Tilt the skillet to spread out the eggs. When edges of the omelet begin to set, draw the edges gently toward the center with a fork.

Tilt the skillet to let the uncooked eggs flow to the edge to cook.

When the omelet is set, spoon on top

> 1 or 2 tablespoons of your favorite jelly or jam

Loosen the edges of the omelet with a fork or pancake turner.

With the help of an adult, hold the handle of the skillet upwards, fold over the omelet and roll it onto a plate.

TO MICROWAVE: Beat eggs and salt as directed above. Place margarine in microwavable pie plate, 9 × 1¼ inches. Set the pie plate on a microwavable dinner plate turned upside down in the microwave.

Microwave uncovered on high (100%) 30 seconds or until margarine is melted; tilt pie plate so the margarine covers the inside of the pie plate.

Pour beaten eggs into pie plate; cover with waxed paper. Microwave on high (100%) 2 to 2 minutes and 30 seconds, moving outer edge of omelet to center and gently shaking pie plate to distribute egg evenly after 1 minute, until center is set but still moist. Finish as directed above.

HINT: *Use a nonstick skillet if you have one. The omelet will come out of the pan much more easily.*

Edie *said she made only one small change to Jelly Omelet. "I put more jelly in because 2 tablespoons wasn't enough." Good idea, Edie!*

*E*gg in a Frame

1 serving

INGREDIENTS

- Bread
- Margarine or butter
- Egg
- Salt

UTENSILS

- Ruler or biscuit cutter
- Table knife
- 8-inch skillet with lid
- Pancake turner
- Measuring cup or saucer

Tear a circle about 2½ inches in diameter or cut out center with biscuit cutter from

> 1 slice bread

Spread generously on both sides of bread

> margarine or butter, softened

Put bread "frame" in skillet. Cook over medium heat 4 to 5 minutes or until golden brown on the bottom. Turn bread over, using pancake turner.

Break into measuring cup or saucer

> 1 egg

Carefully slip egg into circle. Turn heat down; cover pan. Cook over low heat 5 to 7 minutes or until white is set, a film forms over yolks and yolks are thickened.

Sprinkle lightly with

> salt

Lift from skillet, using pancake turner.

Egg in a Frame

*M*orning Muffin Meal

4 servings

INGREDIENTS

- English muffins
- Sausage patties
- Shake-'em-up Scrambled Eggs (page 34)

UTENSILS

- Sharp knife
- Cutting board
- Toaster
- Pancake turner
- Dry measuring cup

Cut in half

> 4 English muffins

Toast muffin halves on medium toaster setting.

Cook according to the directions on the package

> 4 sausage patties

Follow the directions on page 34 to cook

> Shake-'em-up Scrambled Eggs, leaving out the tomatoes and cheese

To assemble each muffin, top 1 half of each toasted English muffin with about ¼ cup of scrambled eggs. Put 1 sausage patty on top of scrambled egg. Top with other half of English muffin.

Jeremy *came up with the title for this recipe, Morning Muffin Meal.*

Wonderful Waffles

6 to 8 waffles

INGREDIENTS

- Eggs
- Buttermilk
- Flour
- Baking powder
- Baking soda
- Shortening
- Margarine or butter
- Syrup

UTENSILS

- Waffle iron
- Medium bowl
- Liquid measuring cup
- Dry measuring cups
- Measuring spoons
- Eggbeater
- Fork

Heat waffle iron.

Beat in medium bowl with eggbeater until smooth

> 2 eggs
> 2 cups buttermilk
> 2 cups all-purpose flour
> 2 teaspoons baking powder
> 1 teaspoon baking soda
> 6 tablespoons shortening

Pour about ⅓ cup batter onto center of hot waffle iron. Bake about 5 minutes or until steaming stops.

Remove waffle carefully with fork. Repeat until batter is gone.

Serve hot with

> margarine or butter and your favorite syrup

Favorite French Toast

6 servings

INGREDIENTS

- Shortening
- Eggs
- Milk
- Salt
- Bread
- Powdered sugar or syrup

UTENSILS

- Griddle or electric skillet
- Small bowl
- Liquid measuring cup
- Measuring spoons
- Fork
- Pancake turner

Grease griddle or electric skillet with shortening if necessary.

Heat griddle over medium heat or heat electric skillet to 375°. (To test griddle, sprinkle with a few drops of water. If bubbles skitter around, heat is just right.)

Mix in small bowl with fork

> 2 eggs
> ½ cup milk
> ¼ teaspoon salt

Dip into egg mixture

> 6 slices day-old bread

Cook bread on hot griddle about 4 minutes or until golden brown on the bottom (lift an edge and peek).

Turn bread over using pancake turner and cook about 4 minutes on other side.

Serve with

> powdered sugar or your favorite syrup

*F*rench Toast Sandwiches

4 servings

INGREDIENTS

- Shortening
- Bread
- Soft cream cheese
- Jam or jelly
- Eggs
- Milk
- Vanilla
- Powdered sugar
- Maple-flavored syrup or your favorite topping

UTENSILS

- Griddle or electric skillet
- Measuring spoons
- Table knife
- Large bowl
- Liquid measuring cup
- Eggbeater
- Pancake turner

Grease griddle or electric skillet with shortening if necessary.

Heat griddle over medium heat or heat electric skillet to 375°. (To test griddle, sprinkle with a few drops of water. If bubbles skitter around, heat is just right.)

Spread on each of 4 slices of bread

> 1 tablespoon soft cream cheese
> 2 teaspoons your favorite jam or jelly

Top each with another slice of bread.

Mix together in large bowl with eggbeater

> 3 eggs
> ⅔ cup milk
> ½ teaspoon vanilla

Dip each sandwich, one at a time, into the egg mixture.

Cook sandwiches on hot griddle about 3 minutes or until golden brown on bottom.

Turn with pancake turner and cook about 3 minutes on the other side.

Sprinkle each sandwich with

> powdered sugar

Cut sandwiches into halves or fourths.

Serve with

> maple-flavored syrup or your favorite topping

*A*lphabet Pancakes

About 18 pancakes

INGREDIENTS

- Shortening
- Variety baking mix
- Eggs
- Milk
- Syrup

UTENSILS

- Griddle or electric skillet
- Medium bowl
- Dry measuring cups
- Liquid measuring cup
- Eggbeater
- Teaspoon
- Pancake turner

Grease griddle or electric skillet with shortening if necessary.

Heat griddle over medium heat or heat electric skillet to 375°. (To test griddle, sprinkle with a few drops of water. If bubbles skitter around, heat is just right.)

Beat in medium bowl with eggbeater

> 2 cups variety baking mix
> 2 eggs
> 1 cup milk

Drizzle batter from a teaspoon onto hot griddle to form an initial. (Initials must be made backwards to make them appear "right" when pancakes are served.)

When bottom side of initial has browned, pour about ¼ cup batter over initial.

Cook until edges are dry. Turn and cook until golden. Repeat until the batter is gone.

Serve with

> your favorite syrup

*B*ig Puffy Pancake

4 servings

INGREDIENTS

- Margarine or butter
- Flour
- Milk
- Eggs
- Salt
- Margarine
- Fresh fruit
- Powdered sugar
- Maple-flavored syrup

UTENSILS

- Pie plate, 10 × 1½ inches
- Potholders
- Medium bowl
- Dry measuring cups
- Liquid measuring cup
- Measuring spoons
- Eggbeater
- Rubber scraper
- Sharp knife

Heat oven to 425°.

Put in pie plate

> 3 tablespoons margarine or butter

Heat in oven just until the margarine is melted. (Ask an adult to help you.)

Remove pan from oven.

Mix together in medium bowl with eggbeater until smooth

> ½ cup all-purpose flour
> ½ cup milk
> 4 eggs
> ⅛ teaspoon salt

Beat in

> melted margarine

Pour mixture into pie plate.

Bake the pancake about 25 minutes or until it is puffy and golden brown. (Have an adult help you take the pancake out of the oven. It will be very hot!)

Top pancake with

> your favorite fresh fruit

Sprinkle with

> powdered sugar

Cut into 4 wedges

Serve with

> maple-flavored syrup

BIG PUFFY BLUEBERRY PANCAKE: Fold in ½ cup fresh or frozen (thawed and drained) blueberries into batter before pouring into pie plate.

*B*anana Pancakes

About 18 pancakes

INGREDIENTS

- Shortening
- Bananas
- Variety baking mix
- Milk
- Sugar
- Egg
- Honey or jelly

UTENSILS

- Griddle or electric skillet
- Small bowl
- Fork
- Medium bowl
- Dry measuring cups
- Liquid measuring cup
- Measuring spoons
- Eggbeater
- Rubber scraper
- Pancake turner

Grease griddle or electric skillet with shortening if necessary.

Heat griddle over medium heat or heat electric skillet to 375°. (To test griddle, sprinkle with a few drops of water. If bubbles skitter around, the heat is just right.)

Mash in small bowl with fork

2 medium ripe bananas

Beat in medium bowl with eggbeater

2 cups variety baking mix
1½ cups milk
2 tablespoons sugar
1 egg

Fold mashed banana into batter with rubber scraper.

Pour batter by scant ¼ cupfuls onto hot griddle.

Cook until edges are dry. Turn and cook until golden. Repeat until the batter is gone.

Serve with

honey or your favorite jelly

*Q*uick Cheesy Grits

1 serving

INGREDIENTS

- Salt
- White hominy quick grits
- Shredded Cheddar cheese
- Margarine or butter

UTENSILS

- 1-quart saucepan
- Liquid measuring cup
- Measuring spoons
- Long-handled spoon
- Dry measuring cup

Heat to boiling in saucepan

> 1 cup water
> dash of salt

Stir in, a little at a time

> 3 tablespoons white hominy quick grits

Lower heat and simmer uncovered, stirring often, about 2½ minutes. Remove from heat.

Stir in

> ¼ cup shredded Cheddar cheese (1 ounce)
> 1 teaspoon margarine or butter

Let stand 1 minute to thicken.

Edie *suggested omitting the cheese and sprinkling Quick Cheesy Grits with brown sugar for a sweet twist.*

*H*omemade Pancake Syrup

1¾ cups

INGREDIENTS

- Brown sugar
- Margarine or butter
- Salt
- Maple flavoring

UTENSILS

- 1-quart saucepan
- Dry measuring cups
- Liquid measuring cup
- Large spoon
- Measuring spoons

Mix in saucepan

> 1½ cups packed brown sugar
> ¾ cup water
> 1 tablespoon margarine or butter
> dash of salt

Heat to boiling over medium heat, stirring all the time. Remove the pan from heat.

Stir in

> ½ teaspoon maple flavoring

Serve warm.

Following pages: Toast Toppers (page 54), Lemon-Blueberry Muffins (page 48), Surprise Muffins (page 49), Easy Cinnamon Rolls (page 50)

Lemon-Blueberry Muffins

12 muffins

INGREDIENTS

- Shortening
- Egg
- Variety baking mix
- Sugar
- Vegetable oil
- Lemon-flavored yogurt
- Blueberries

UTENSILS

- Medium muffin cups, $2\frac{1}{2} \times 1\frac{1}{4}$ inches
- Medium bowl
- Fork
- Dry measuring cups
- Measuring spoons
- Long-handled spoon
- Potholders
- Wire cooling rack

Heat oven to 400°.

Grease bottoms of 12 muffin cups with shortening or line with paper baking cups.

Beat slightly in medium bowl with fork

1 egg

Mix in just until moistened (batter should be lumpy)

2 cups variety baking mix ¼ cup sugar 2 tablespoons vegetable oil 1 container (6 ounces) lemon-flavored yogurt

Gently fold into batter

¾ cup fresh or frozen (thawed and drained) blueberries

Fill muffin cups ⅔ full.

Bake 15 to 18 minutes or until golden brown.

Carefully remove muffins from pan right away. Cool on wire rack.

TO MICROWAVE: Prepare Lemon-Blueberry batter as directed above. Place 2 paper baking cups in each cup of 6-cup microwavable muffin ring.

Spoon half of the batter into the baking cups, filling each ⅔ full.

Microwave uncovered on high (100%) 2 to 3 minutes 30 seconds, turning ring ¼ turn every minute, until a wooden pick inserted in the center comes out clean. (Parts of muffins will look a little wet, but they will continue cooking while they stand.)

Cool muffins 1 minute, then remove from ring very carefully. Let stand uncovered on wire rack for 2 minutes.

Use the rest of the batter by repeating these steps.

No fancy words for Lemon-Blueberry Muffins. **Scott** *said straight out, "These muffins are GOOD."*

*S*urprise Muffins

12 muffins

INGREDIENTS

- Shortening
- Egg
- Milk
- Vegetable oil
- Flour
- Sugar
- Baking powder
- Salt
- Jelly

UTENSILS

- Medium muffin cups, 2½ × 1¼ inches
- Medium bowl
- Liquid measuring cup
- Fork
- Dry measuring cups
- Measuring spoons
- Large spoon
- Teaspoon
- Potholders
- Wire cooling rack

Heat oven to 400°.

Grease bottoms of 12 muffin cups with shortening or line with paper baking cups.

Beat in medium bowl with fork

> 1 egg
> ½ cup milk
> ¼ cup vegetable oil

Mix in just until flour is moistened (batter should be lumpy)

> 1½ cups all-purpose flour
> ½ cup sugar
> 2 teaspoons baking powder
> ½ teaspoon salt

Fill muffin cups ½ full.

Drop onto center of each muffin

> 1 teaspoon your favorite jelly

Add batter to fill muffin cups ⅔ full.

Bake 20 to 25 minutes or until golden brown. Carefully remove muffins from pan right away. Cool on wire rack.

TO MICROWAVE: Place 2 paper baking cups in each cup of a 6-cup microwavable muffin ring.

Spoon about 1 slightly rounded tablespoonful of batter into each muffin cup (cups should be about ¼ full). Drop jelly onto center of each muffin. Add about 1 more spoonful batter on top. (Muffin cup should be about half full.)

Mix in small bowl

> 1 tablespoon sugar
> ¼ teaspoon ground cinnamon

Sprinkle a little on top of each muffin.

Microwave uncovered on high (100%) 2 minutes to 3 minutes 30 seconds, turning ring ¼ turn every minute, until tops of muffins are almost dry and wooden pick inserted in center comes out clean. (Parts of muffins will look a little wet, but they will continue cooking while they stand.)

Cool muffins 1 minute, then remove from ring very carefully. Let stand uncovered on wire rack for 2 minutes.

Use the rest of the batter by repeating these steps.

Easy Cinnamon Rolls

12 rolls

INGREDIENTS

- Shortening
- Variety baking mix
- Milk
- Margarine or butter
- Sugar
- Ground cinnamon

UTENSILS

- Medium muffin cups, 2½ × 1¼ inches
- Small bowls
- Rolling pin
- Dry measuring cups
- Liquid measuring cup
- Fork
- Ruler
- Table knife
- Measuring spoons
- Sharp knife
- Potholders

Heat oven to 425°.

Grease 12 muffin cups with shortening.

Mix in a small bowl with fork

2 cups variety baking mix ⅔ cup milk

Sprinkle a clean surface (such as a kitchen counter or breadboard) with baking mix or flour. Place the dough on the floured surface.

Knead dough gently 8 to 10 times. Roll into 12 × 7-inch rectangle.

Spread thinly with

margarine or butter, softened

Mix in another small bowl

¼ cup sugar 1 teaspoon ground cinnamon

Sprinkle dough with cinnamon mixture.

Roll up tightly, starting with the long end. Seal by pinching the dough with your fingers. Cut into 1-inch slices. Put 1 slice in each muffin cup.

Bake about 15 minutes or until brown.

*C*innamon-Raisin Bread

1 loaf

INGREDIENTS

- Frozen white bread dough
- Shortening
- Flour
- Margarine or butter
- Sugar
- Ground cinnamon
- Raisins

UTENSILS

- Loaf pan, 9 × 5 × 3 inches
- Ruler
- Table knife
- Small bowl
- Measuring spoons
- Teaspoon
- Dry measuring cup
- Potholders
- Pastry brush
- Wire cooling rack

Thaw according to the directions on the package

> 1 loaf frozen white bread dough

Generously grease loaf pan with shortening.

Sprinkle a clean surface (such as a kitchen counter or breadboard) lightly with flour. Place the thawed dough on the floured surface. With floured hands or a rolling pin, flatten the dough into a 15 × 7-inch rectangle.

Spread over the dough

> 1 tablespoon margarine or butter, softened

Mix together in small bowl

> 1 tablespoon sugar
> ½ teaspoon ground cinnamon

Sprinkle the cinnamon mixture over the dough.

Sprinkle evenly over the cinnamon mixture

> ½ cup raisins

Starting at one narrow end of the rectangle, tightly roll up dough. Seal by pinching dough with your fingers.

Place dough, seam side down, in greased loaf pan. Cover and let dough rise in a warm place (85°) about 3½ to 4 hours until dough fills pan.

Heat oven to 350°.

Bake 25 to 35 minutes or until bread is deep golden brown and sounds hollow when tapped. Ask an adult to remove bread from loaf pan.

Using pastry brush, brush top of hot loaf with a little margarine or butter. Cool bread on wire rack.

Jenna *tackled the Cinnamon-Raisin Bread like a pro and received rave reviews from her family. She told us, "They thought it looked like I bought it at a bakery."*

Scones

8 scones

INGREDIENTS

- Shortening
- Variety baking mix
- Milk
- Sugar
- Egg
- Margarine or butter
- Jam

UTENSILS

- Cookie sheet
- Medium bowl
- Dry measuring cup
- Liquid measuring cup
- Measuring spoons
- Long-handled spoon
- Ruler
- Pastry brush
- Sharp knife
- Potholders
- Pancake turner

Heat oven to 425°.

Grease cookie sheet with shortening.

Mix together in medium bowl until dough forms

> 2 cups variety baking mix
> ⅓ cup milk
> 3 tablespoons sugar
> 1 egg

Sprinkle a clean surface (such as a kitchen counter or breadboard) lightly with baking mix or flour. Place dough on the floured surface.

Roll ball of dough around 3 or 4 times. Knead quickly and lightly by folding, pressing and turning. Repeat 10 times.

Pat dough into 8-inch circle on cookie sheet. (If dough is sticky, dip your fingers in flour or baking mix before patting.)

Using pastry brush, brush dough lightly with

> milk

Sprinkle with

> ½ teaspoon sugar

Cut dough into 8 wedges. (Leave wedges in circle.) Bake about 12 minutes or until golden brown.

Carefully separate wedges with pancake turner.

Serve the scones with

> margarine or butter and jam

CURRANT SCONES: Stir ¼ cup currants into dough mixture. (Currants look and taste like tiny raisins.)

*C*innamon-Apple Toast

1 serving

INGREDIENTS	UTENSILS
■ Apple	■ Sharp knife
■ Bread	■ Cutting board
■ Margarine or butter	■ Table knife
■ Sugar	■ Cookie sheet
■ Ground cinnamon	■ Measuring spoons
	■ Potholders
	■ Plate
	■ Pancake turner

Heat oven to 375°.

Wash and cut into thin slices

> ½ small apple

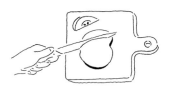

Remove seeds from apple slices.

Spread on 1 slice of bread

> 1 teaspoon margarine or butter

Put bread on cookie sheet buttered side up. Place apple slices on bread.

Sprinkle on top of apples

> 1 teaspoon sugar
> a few dashes of ground cinnamon

Bake about 15 minutes or until bread is toasted. Carefully remove cookie sheet from oven.

Place toast on plate with pancake turner.

*T*oast Toppers

Jelly or Jam

Spread hot buttered toast with jellied cranberry sauce, currant jelly or orange marmalade. Sprinkle with powdered sugar.

Caramel-Coconut Spread

Mix 2 tablespoons packed brown sugar, 2 tablespoons flaked coconut and 1 tablespoon margarine or butter, softened. Spread on hot unbuttered toast. Toast under broiler until it bubbles (watch carefully).

Cinnamon Mix

Combine 2 tablespoons sugar and 1 teaspoon cinnamon. Sprinkle on hot buttered toast. Cut toast into strips.

Raisin–Peanut Butter

Mix ¼ cup peanut butter, 2 tablespoons chopped seedless raisins and 2 tablespoons orange juice. Spread on hot buttered toast. Cut the toast into 2 triangles.

*H*oney-glazed Grapefruit

2 servings

INGREDIENTS

- Grapefruit
- Honey or maple syrup
- Maraschino cherries

UTENSILS

- Sharp knife
- Cutting board
- Measuring spoons
- Serrated grapefruit spoon

Cut in half

1 grapefruit

Drizzle over each grapefruit half

1 teaspoon honey or maple syrup

Place in center of each grapefruit half

1 maraschino cherry

Eat grapefruit with a serrated grapefruit spoon.

BROILED HONEY-GLAZED GRAPEFRUITS:

Ask an adult to help you do this.

Set oven control to broil.

Place grapefruit halves (without cherries) on cookie sheet.

Broil grapefruits with tops 4 to 6 inches from heat 5 to 10 minutes or until juice bubbles and edge of peel turns light brown.

Carefully remove from oven. Place a cherry in center of each grapefruit half.

TO MICROWAVE: Place grapefruit halves (without cherries) on microwavable plate. Microwave uncovered on high (100%) about 3 minutes or until juice bubbles. Place a cherry in center of each grapefruit half.

HINT: *If you don't have a serrated grapefruit spoon, ask an adult to cut around the edge and sections to loosen the grapefruit from the peel. Do this before drizzling with honey.*

Katie *enjoyed Honey-glazed Grapefruit and learned what "serrated" means. In case you're not sure, a serrated grapefruit spoon has sharp edges to cut through the grapefruit sections.*

Noontime Fixin's

3

Hungry-time Hoagies (page 63)

Sunny Chicken Salad Sandwiches

4 servings

INGREDIENTS

- Celery
- Canned chunk chicken
- Mayonnaise or salad dressing
- Lemon juice
- Curry powder, if you like
- Salt
- Bread

UTENSILS

- Sharp knife
- Cutting board
- Can opener
- Colander
- Fork
- Small bowl
- Dry measuring cup
- Measuring spoons
- Long-handled spoon
- Table knife

Wash and cut into thin slices

1 stalk celery

Drain in colander

1 can (6¾ ounces) chunk chicken

Break apart chicken with fork. Put the chicken and celery in small bowl.

Stir in

¼ cup mayonnaise or salad dressing 1 tablespoon lemon juice ½ to 1 teaspoon curry powder ¼ teaspoon salt

Spread equal amounts of the chicken mixture on

4 slices bread

Top each with another slice of bread.

Cut sandwiches into halves or quarters. Serve with pickles if you like. Refrigerate any leftover sandwiches.

*Beside the taste, **Ryan** enjoyed Sunny Chicken Salad Sandwiches because "the recipe was very easy to understand and it took little time." Fast and fantastic!*

Watermelon Star Salad (page 73), Sunny Chicken Salad Sandwiches

Vegetable Patch Pita Sandwiches

4 servings

INGREDIENTS

- Fresh vegetables
- Mayonnaise or salad dressing
- Prepared mustard
- Pita bread

UTENSILS

- Medium bowl
- Sharp knife
- Cutting board
- Dry measuring cups
- Measuring spoons
- Long-handled spoon
- Teaspoon

Mix together in medium bowl

3 cups bite-size cut-up fresh vegetables
Choose at least two of the following vegetables:
cauliflower
broccoli
carrots
green bell pepper
green onion
cherry tomatoes
zucchini
½ cup mayonnaise or salad dressing
1 teaspoon prepared mustard

Cut in half crosswise

4 six-inch pita breads

Open "pocket" in each pita bread half. Spoon about ⅓ cup of the vegetable mixture into each pita bread pocket.

Edie *and her family loved the Vegetable Patch Pita Sandwiches. She did share one bit of advice with us. "I think it would be very good to put in a cookbook." Here it is, Edie.*

*H*ard-cooked Eggs

INGREDIENTS   **UTENSILS**

- Eggs
- Saucepan with lid
- Ruler

Put in saucepan

desired number of eggs

Add enough cold water to come at least 1 inch above eggs. Heat rapidly to boiling; remove from heat. Cover and let stand 18 minutes.

Run cold water into the pan to quickly cool the eggs and prevent further cooking.

When eggs are cool enough to handle, tap each egg on the kitchen counter to crack shell. Roll egg between your hands to loosen shell, then peel. Hold egg under running water to help rinse off the shell.

*E*gg Salad Sandwiches

4 sandwiches

INGREDIENTS   **UTENSILS**

- Hard-cooked eggs (left)
- Celery
- Mayonnaise or salad dressing
- Onion salt
- Bread

- Sharp knife
- Cutting board
- Medium bowl
- Measuring spoons
- Spoon
- Table knife

Follow the directions on this page to cook

3 hard-cooked eggs

Peel the eggs and chop them into small pieces.

Wash and chop into very small pieces

1 stalk celery

Put chopped eggs and celery in medium bowl.

Stir in

3 tablespoons mayonnaise or salad dressing ¼ teaspoon onion salt

Spread 4 slices of bread with the egg mixture and cover each with another slice of bread to make 4 sandwiches. Cut each sandwich in half and serve right away. Refrigerate any leftover sandwiches.

*C*hunky Tuna Sandwiches

6 sandwiches

INGREDIENTS

- Canned tuna
- Celery
- Dill or sweet pickle
- Mayonnaise or salad dressing
- Onion salt
- Lemon juice
- Margarine or butter
- Bread

UTENSILS

- Can opener
- Medium bowl
- Strainer
- Sharp knife
- Cutting board
- Dry measuring cup
- Measuring spoons
- Fork
- Table knife

Drain and place in medium bowl

> 1 can (6½ ounces) tuna

Wash and chop and place in bowl

> 1 stalk celery

Chop and place in same bowl

> 1 large dill or sweet pickle

Stir with fork into tuna, celery and pickle

> ¼ cup mayonnaise or salad dressing
> ¼ teaspoon onion salt
> ¼ teaspoon lemon juice

Spread with softened margarine or butter

> 12 slices bread

Spread 6 slices of bread with the tuna mixture and cover with remaining slices. Cut sandwiches into halves or quarters. Serve with pickles if you like. Refrigerate any leftovers.

HOT TUNA SANDWICHES: Heat oven to 375°.

Use 3 hamburger buns, cut in half, in place of the bread. Place the buns on a cookie sheet.

Omit the margarine. Spread each bun half with about ⅙ of the tuna mixture.

Wash 1 medium tomato and cut it into 6 slices. Place 1 slice on each bun half and sprinkle with salt.

Cover each tomato slice with 1 slice process American cheese and sprinkle with paprika.

Bake 8 minutes or until the cheese melts.

*H*ungry-time Hoagies

6 sandwiches

INGREDIENTS

- Hoagie or hot dog buns
- Mayonnaise or salad dressing
- Tomatoes
- Sliced ham, luncheon meat or roast beef
- Sliced cheese
- Lettuce

UTENSILS

- Sharp knife
- Cutting board
- Table knife

If not already split, cut in half lengthwise

6 hoagie or hot dog buns

Spread each split hoagie bun with

mayonnaise or salad dressing

Wash and slice

2 medium tomatoes

Place on each hoagie bun

2 or 3 slices of ham, luncheon meat or roast beef 1 slice cheese 2 slices of tomato 1 piece lettuce

HINT: *For easier eating, cut Hungry-time Hoagies in half crosswise. You can add mustard to your hoagie if you like.*

Jenna *said "No tomatoes" on her Hungry-time Hoagies. She prepared this yummy sandwich her way —without tomatoes. You can build your hoagie with any of your favorite cold cuts—and vegetables too!*

*T*oasty Hot Dog Roll-ups

8 roll-ups

INGREDIENTS	UTENSILS
■ Margarine or butter	■ 1-quart saucepan
■ Bread	■ Cookie sheet
■ Prepared mustard	■ Pastry brush
■ Process American cheese	■ Table knife
■ Hot dogs	■ Measuring spoons
■ Ketchup	■ Wooden picks
	■ Potholders

Heat oven to 375°.

Melt in saucepan over low heat (ask an adult to help you)

½ cup margarine or butter

Place on cookie sheet

8 slices bread

Using pastry brush, brush the bread slices with about half of the melted margarine.

Spread with

2 teaspoons prepared mustard

Cut in half so you have 8 cheese triangles

4 slices process American cheese

Top each bread slice with 1 cheese triangle. Place 1 hot dog on each cheese triangle. Fold the bread over to make a triangle shape. Fasten each with 2 wooden picks, one on each side, poking them through the bread and hot dog. Brush the outside of the bread triangles with remaining melted margarine. Bake 10 to 15 minutes or until golden brown.

Serve with

ketchup

Toasty Hot Dog Roll-ups, Chocolate Milk Shake (page 12)

*L*ittle Lunch Pizzas

1 serving

INGREDIENTS

- English muffin
- Pizza sauce
- Shredded Cheddar or mozzarella cheese

UTENSILS

- Sharp knife
- Cutting board
- Toaster
- Cookie sheet
- Measuring spoons
- Potholders
- Pancake turner
- Plate

Heat oven to 425°.

Cut in half

1 English muffin

Toast muffin halves on medium toaster setting. Put muffin halves on cookie sheet.

Top each muffin half with

1 tablespoon pizza sauce 1 tablespoon shredded Cheddar or mozzarella cheese

Bake in oven about 5 minutes or until cheese is melted.

Use pancake turner to place on plate.

TO MICROWAVE: Toast English muffin halves, top with pizza sauce and cheese as directed above.

Put a microwavable paper towel on microwavable plate. Place muffin halves on the paper towel. Microwave uncovered on high (100%) 30 to 45 seconds or until cheese is melted.

Cool slightly before eating.

HINT: *For a heartier pizza, try adding some sliced olives, crumbled cooked hamburger, chopped tomato, sliced pepperoni or your favorite topping before putting cheese on muffin half.*

*H*earty Whole Wheat Bread

1 loaf

INGREDIENTS

- Shortening
- Active dry yeast
- All-purpose flour
- Whole wheat flour
- Honey, packed brown sugar or light molasses
- Salt
- Margarine or butter

UTENSILS

- Loaf pan, 9 × 5 × 3 inches
- Large bowl
- Liquid measuring cup
- Dry measuring cups
- Measuring spoons
- Electric mixer
- Large spoon
- Rubber scraper
- Ruler
- Potholders
- Wire cooling rack
- Pastry brush

Grease loaf pan with shortening.

Dissolve in 1¼ cups warm water in large bowl

> 1 package active dry yeast

Add

> ½ cup all-purpose flour
> 1 cup whole wheat flour
> 2 tablespoons honey, packed brown sugar or light molasses
> 2 tablespoons shortening
> 2 teaspoons salt

Beat 2 minutes on medium speed of electric mixer, scraping bowl often. (By hand, beat 300 vigorous strokes.)

Beat in remaining 1½ cups all-purpose flour with spoon until smooth, 1 to 1½ minutes. Scrape batter from side of bowl.

Cover; let rise in warm place about 45 minutes or until double.

Stir down batter by beating about 25 strokes (batter will be sticky). Spread batter in greased pan.

Smooth top of loaf by patting with floured hands. Let rise about 45 minutes or until batter is 1 inch from top of the pan.

Heat oven to 375°.

Bake 45 to 50 minutes or until loaf is brown and sounds hollow when tapped.

Remove bread from pan right away. Brush top with

> melted margarine or butter

Cool on wire rack. Cool thoroughly before cutting.

Very Vegetable Soup

6 servings

INGREDIENTS

- Condensed chicken broth
- Stewed tomatoes
- Frozen mixed vegetables
- Dried oregano
- Dried thyme
- Pepper
- Macaroni rings

UTENSILS

- 3-quart saucepan
- Can opener
- Measuring spoons
- Long-handled spoon
- Dry measuring cup

Mix together in saucepan

> 1 can (10¾ ounces) condensed chicken broth
> 1 soup can water
> 1 can (14½ ounces) stewed tomatoes, undrained
> 1 package (10 ounces) frozen mixed vegetables, separated
> ¼ teaspoon dried oregano
> ¼ teaspoon dried thyme
> ⅛ teaspoon pepper

Break up tomatoes with spoon.

Heat mixture to boiling; lower heat and simmer 10 minutes.

Stir in

> ½ cup uncooked macaroni rings

Cook 8 minutes or until macaroni is tender.

TO MICROWAVE: Mix all ingredients except the macaroni in 3-quart microwavable casserole.

Cover with lid or plastic wrap. If using plastic wrap, turn back 1 edge to make a little space for steam to come out.

Microwave on high (100%) 5 minutes.

Carefully remove lid and stir. Replace lid and microwave on high (100%) 8 to 10 minutes or until boiling.

Carefully remove lid. Stir in macaroni. Replace lid and microwave on high (100%) 6 to 8 minutes or until macaroni is tender.

HINT: *You can separate frozen vegetables by placing them in cool water.*

Very Vegetable Soup, Hearty Whole Wheat Bread (page 67)

*C*hicken Noodle Soup

4 servings

INGREDIENTS

- Condensed chicken broth
- Egg noodles
- Parsley
- Cooked or canned chunk chicken

UTENSILS

- Can opener
- 3-quart saucepan
- Dry measuring cup
- Scissors
- Measuring spoons
- Long-handled spoon

Prepare according to the directions on the can

> 2 cans (10¾ ounces) condensed chicken broth

Heat to boiling.

Add

> 2 cups uncooked egg noodles

Cook over medium-high heat 6 to 8 minutes or until noodles are tender.

Rinse and snip with scissors

> 1 tablespoon fresh parsley

Just before serving, stir in parsley and

> 1 cup cooked cut-up chicken or 1 can (6¾ ounces) chunk chicken, drained

*Q*uick Tomato Soup with Rice

4 servings

INGREDIENTS

- Condensed tomato soup
- Instant rice

UTENSILS

- 2-quart saucepan with lid
- Can opener
- Dry measuring cup
- Large spoon

Prepare according to the directions on the can using water

> 1 can (10¾ ounces) condensed tomato soup

Heat soup to boiling.

Stir in

> 1 cup uncooked instant rice

Cover pan and remove from heat. Let stand 5 minutes; stir.

𝒞runchy Tortellini Salad

6 to 8 servings

INGREDIENTS

- Dried tortellini
- Carrot
- Celery
- Tomato
- Pitted ripe olives, if you like
- Italian salad dressing
- Grated Parmesan cheese

UTENSILS

- 3-quart saucepan
- Colander
- Medium bowl
- Vegetable parer
- Sharp knife
- Cutting board
- Dry measuring cup
- Liquid measuring cup
- Measuring spoons
- Long-handled spoon
- Plastic wrap

Cook in saucepan according to the directions on the package

> 1 package (7 ounces) dried tortellini, any flavor

Drain the cooked tortellini in colander. Put tortellini in medium bowl.

Wash, pare and slice

> 1 carrot

Wash and slice

> 1 stalk celery

Wash and chop

> 1 medium tomato

Carefully mix with the tortellini, the carrot, celery, tomato and

> ½ cup pitted ripe olives
> ½ cup Italian salad dressing
> 2 tablespoons grated Parmesan cheese

Cover the bowl with plastic wrap and refrigerate about 2 hours or until chilled.

*B*unny Salad

4 servings

INGREDIENTS

- Lettuce
- Canned pear halves
- Sliced almonds
- Raisins
- Red cinnamon candies
- Cottage cheese

UTENSILS

- Paper towel
- Salad plates
- Can opener
- Measuring spoons

Wash, pat dry with paper towel and shred

lettuce

Put 1 lettuce leaf on each salad plate.

Put, cut side down, on each lettuce leaf

1 canned pear half

Arrange on the narrow end of each pear half to form bunny face

2 sliced almonds and 2 raisins for eyes 1 red cinnamon candy for nose 2 sliced almonds for ears

Place at opposite end of each pear half

2 tablespoons cottage cheese

Bunny Salad

*W*atermelon Star Salad

1 serving

INGREDIENTS

- Lettuce leaf
- Watermelon
- Creamed cottage cheese
- Blueberries

UTENSILS

- Paper towel
- Salad plate
- Sharp knife
- Cutting board
- Ruler
- Teaspoon
- Dry measuring cup
- Measuring spoons

Wash and pat dry with paper towel

1 lettuce leaf

Place lettuce leaf on salad plate.

Cut into 5 wedges

½ slice watermelon, 1 inch thick

Trim red melon away from white part and green rind. On lettuce leaf, arrange melon wedges in a circle with the points outward to form a star.

Spoon into the center of the watermelon star

½ cup creamed cottage cheese

Wash and sprinkle over the cottage cheese

1 tablespoon blueberries

Dinner Delights

4

Smiling Face Pizzas (page 76)

$\mathcal{S}$miling Face Pizzas

4 pizzas

INGREDIENTS

- Tomato sauce
- Ground beef
- Dry bread crumbs
- Dried oregano
- Pitted ripe olives
- Shredded mozzarella cheese
- Shredded Cheddar cheese
- Sliced pimientos

UTENSILS

- Can opener
- Liquid measuring cup
- Medium bowl
- Dry measuring cup
- Measuring spoons
- Fork
- Jelly roll pan, 15½ × 10½ × 1 inch
- Ruler
- Rubber scraper
- Sharp knife
- Cutting board
- Potholders

Heat oven to 425°.

Measure and put in medium bowl ½ cup from

1 can (8 ounces) tomato sauce

Save the rest of the sauce.

Add to bowl and mix with fork

1 pound ground beef ½ cup dry bread crumbs ½ teaspoon dried oregano

Divide the ground beef mixture into 4 equal parts. Place several inches apart in jelly roll pan.

Pat each part into a 4½-inch circle. Pinch the edge of each circle to make a little stand-up rim.

Pour about 2 tablespoons of the remaining tomato sauce into the center of each circle and spread it to the edge with a rubber scraper. Bake 15 to 20 minutes.

While the pizzas are baking, cut crosswise into 4 slices each

2 pitted ripe olives

Remove the pan from oven and turn oven off.

To form face, sprinkle each pizza with

2 tablespoons shredded mozzarella cheese

For hair, sprinkle around the edge

2 tablespoons shredded Cheddar cheese

Use the olive slices for eyes. For the mouth, use

4 pimiento slices

Return pizzas to warm oven and heat about 5 minutes or until cheese melts.

HINT: *Be creative and use your favorite foods to make all types of faces.*

*T*op It Your Way Pizza

4 servings

INGREDIENTS

- Shortening
- Frozen pizza dough, thawed
- Pizza sauce
- Pizza Toppings (right)
- Shredded mozzarella cheese

UTENSILS

- Cookie sheet or 15-inch pizza pan
- Ruler
- Can opener
- Rubber scraper
- Sharp knife
- Cutting board
- Dry measuring cups
- Potholders

Heat oven to 350°.

Grease cookie sheet or pizza pan with shortening.

Shape into 14 × 11-inch rectangle or a circle on cookie sheet

> 1 loaf of thawed frozen pizza dough

Spread over the dough with rubber scraper

> 1 can (8 ounces) pizza sauce

Sprinkle 2 or 3 Pizza Toppings over the sauce.

PIZZA TOPPINGS

1 cup sliced mushrooms
½ cup chopped green bell pepper
¼ cup sliced ripe olives
a few thinly sliced onion rings
½ of a 3½-ounce package thinly sliced pepperoni
¼ pound hamburger or sausage, cooked and crumbled
your favorite topping

Sprinkle over the toppings

> 1½ cups shredded mozzarella cheese

Bake on lowest oven rack 25 to 35 minutes or until cheese is melted and light brown.

Scott *loves pizza! So Top It Your Way Pizza was perfect for Scott, and he did top it his way—with hot dogs!*

*J*uicy Hamburgers

6 hamburgers

INGREDIENTS

- Onion
- Ground beef
- Worcestershire sauce
- Salt
- Pepper

UTENSILS

- Sharp knife
- Cutting board
- Medium bowl
- Liquid measuring cup
- Measuring spoons
- Fork
- Ruler
- Broiler pan
- Pancake turner

Wash and chop

> 1 small onion

Mix with fork in medium bowl, onion and

> 1½ pounds ground beef
> ¼ cup water
> 1 teaspoon Worcestershire sauce
> ¼ teaspoon salt
> ¼ teaspoon pepper

Shape mixture with your hands into 6 burgers, each about ¾ inch thick.

Set oven control to broil. Broil with tops about 3 inches from heat for 5 minutes.

Turn burgers over with pancake turner. Broil 5 to 7 minutes longer.

*T*acos

10 tacos

INGREDIENTS

- Lettuce
- Tomato
- Shredded Cheddar cheese
- Ground beef
- Taco seasoning mix
- Canned refried beans
- Taco shells
- Bottled taco sauce

UTENSILS

- Cutting board
- Sharp knife
- Small serving bowls
- 10-inch skillet
- Long-handled spoons
- Strainer
- 2-quart saucepan
- Can opener
- Potholders
- Serving platter
- Large serving bowl
- Serving spoons
- Teaspoons

Wash and chop into long shreds

> 1 lettuce wedge (about 1 inch thick)

Place the lettuce in a small serving bowl.

Wash and cut stem end from

> 1 large tomato

Chop into ¼-inch pieces. Place chopped tomato in another small serving bowl.

Empty into a third small serving bowl

> 1 package (4 ounces) shredded Cheddar cheese (1 cup)

Heat oven to temperature given on taco shell package

Crumble into skillet

1 pound ground beef

Cook and stir over medium heat about 10 minutes or until brown. Pour beef into strainer to drain off any fat. Put beef back in skillet.

Prepare according to package directions, add to the beef

1 package (1.51 ounces) taco seasoning mix

(Do not put beef in taco shells yet.)

While the beef mixture is simmering, heat in saucepan until heated through

2 cans (16 ounces each) refried beans

Stir beans often so they don't burn.

Prepare according to package directions

10 taco shells

Put taco shells on serving platter.

Pour the beef mixture into large serving bowl. Serve with the taco shells, lettuce, tomato and cheese.

Let each person assemble his or her own taco. Serve with refried beans and

taco sauce

HINT: *Use mini taco shells to make bite-size tacos for dinner or snacks.*

Sloppy Joes

6 sandwiches

INGREDIENTS

- Celery
- Onion
- Ground beef
- Pepper
- Spaghetti sauce
- Hamburger buns

UTENSILS

- Sharp knife
- Cutting board
- 12-inch skillet
- Long-handled spoon
- Strainer
- Measuring spoons
- Cookie sheet
- Potholders
- Pancake turner
- Serving platter

Wash and chop

> 1 stalk celery
> 1 medium onion

Crumble into skillet with celery and onion

> 1 pound ground beef

Cook and stir over medium-high heat about 10 minutes or until brown. Pour beef into strainer to drain off any fat. Put beef back in skillet.

Stir into ground beef mixture

> ⅛ teaspoon pepper
> 1 jar (16 ounces) spaghetti sauce

Heat to boiling, stirring all the time. Reduce heat. Simmer uncovered over low heat 10 minutes, stirring a few times.

Cut in half crosswise

> 6 hamburger buns

Set oven control to broil. Place bun halves, cut side up, on cookie sheet. Place cookie sheet so tops of the buns will be 4 to 5 inches from heat. Toast buns until light brown. Watch carefully—it will take just 1 to 2 minutes.

Lift the buns to serving platter, using pancake turner. Spoon ground beef mixture onto half of each bun and cover with other half.

TO MICROWAVE: Crumble ground beef into very small pieces in 2-quart microwavable casserole or bowl. Add chopped celery and onion. Cover with waxed paper. (Place waxed paper on casserole so it curls down instead of up. It will stay on better.) Microwave on high (100%) 3 minutes. Carefully remove waxed paper and stir beef. Re-cover and microwave on high 3 to 4 minutes longer or until very little pink is left in the beef.

Pour beef mixture into large strainer to drain off the fat. Put beef mixture back in casserole. Stir in pepper and spaghetti sauce. Cover with lid or plastic wrap. If using plastic wrap, turn back 1 edge to make a little space for steam to come out. Microwave on high (100%) 4 to 5 minutes longer or until hot. Carefully remove lid and stir. Toast hamburger buns as directed above or just spoon Sloppy Joes into buns.

Tacos (page 78), Sloppy Joes

iesta Chili

4 to 6 servings

INGREDIENTS

- Onion
- Ground beef
- Chili powder
- Garlic salt
- Red pepper sauce
- Canned tomatoes
- Canned red kidney beans
- Shredded Cheddar cheese

UTENSILS

- Sharp knife
- Cutting board
- 3-quart saucepan
- Long-handled spoon
- Strainer
- Measuring spoons
- Can opener
- Soup ladle
- Soup bowls

Wash and chop

1 medium onion

Crumble into saucepan with onion

1 pound ground beef

Cook and stir ground beef and onion over medium heat about 10 minutes or until ground beef is brown. Pour into strainer to drain off any fat. Put beef and onion back in saucepan.

Stir in

1 tablespoon chili powder ½ teaspoon garlic salt dash of red pepper sauce 1 can (14½ ounces) tomatoes, undrained

Heat mixture to boiling. Lower heat and simmer 30 minutes, stirring a few times.

Stir in

1 can (16 ounces) red kidney beans, undrained

Cook 30 minutes longer.

Ladle chili into soup bowls.

Top each serving with

1 or 2 tablespoons shredded Cheddar cheese

Quick Cheeseburger Pie

6 servings

INGREDIENTS

- Shortening
- Onions
- Ground beef
- Pepper
- Milk
- Eggs
- Variety baking mix
- Tomatoes
- Shredded Cheddar or process American cheese

UTENSILS

- Pie plate, 10 × 1½ inches
- Sharp knife
- Cutting board
- 10-inch skillet
- Measuring spoons
- Long-handled spoon
- Strainer
- Blender, eggbeater or wire whisk
- Liquid measuring cup
- Dry measuring cups
- Potholders
- Table knife
- Wire cooling rack

Heat oven to 400°.

Grease pie plate with shortening.

Wash and chop

2 medium onions

Put in skillet along with chopped onion

1 pound ground beef
¼ teaspoon pepper

Cook and stir over medium heat about 10 minutes or until brown. Pour beef mixture into strainer to drain off any fat. Spread beef mixture in pie plate.

Put in blender container and blend on high 15 seconds (or use eggbeater or wire whisk)

1½ cups milk
3 eggs
¾ cup variety baking mix

Pour into pie plate. Bake 25 minutes.

Wash and slice

2 medium tomatoes

Carefully take pie out of oven.

Top with tomatoes and sprinkle with

1 cup shredded Cheddar or process American cheese (4 ounces)

Bake 5 to 8 minutes longer or until knife inserted in center comes out clean. Cool 5 minutes on wire rack.

One-Pot Spaghetti

4 to 6 servings

INGREDIENTS

- Ground beef
- Chopped onion
- Canned tomato sauce
- Spaghetti sauce with mushrooms
- Sugar
- Salt
- Spaghetti
- Grated Parmesan cheese

UTENSILS

- Dutch oven
- Long-handled spoon
- Strainer
- Sharp knife
- Cutting board
- Can opener
- Measuring spoons
- Liquid measuring cup

Crumble into Dutch oven

1 pound ground beef

Cook and stir over medium-high heat about 10 minutes or until brown. Pour into strainer to drain off any fat. Put beef back in Dutch oven.

Wash and chop

1 medium onion

Stir into ground beef, the onion and

1 can (8 ounces) tomato sauce 1 jar or can (15 ounces) spaghetti sauce with mushrooms

Add to ground beef mixture

1 teaspoon sugar ½ teaspoon salt 2 cups water 1 package (7 ounces) uncooked long spaghetti

Heat to boiling over medium-high heat, stirring a few times to prevent sticking. Reduce heat. Cover and simmer over low heat about 15 minutes or until the spaghetti is tender. Remove from heat and stir once.

Sprinkle just before serving with

3 tablespoons grated Parmesan cheese

One-Pot Spaghetti, Festive Garlic Bread (page 124)

*F*ootball Meat Loaf

6 servings

INGREDIENTS

- Shortening
- Ground beef
- Dry bread crumbs
- Milk
- Worcestershire sauce
- Dry mustard
- Pepper
- Ground sage
- Onion
- Egg
- Sliced pimientos

UTENSILS

- Rectangular pan, 13 × 9 × 2 inches
- Large bowl
- Dry measuring cup
- Liquid measuring cup
- Measuring spoons
- Sharp knife
- Cutting board
- Long-handled spoon
- Ruler
- Potholders
- Large pancake turners
- Serving platter

Heat oven to 350°.

Grease bottom of rectangular pan with shortening.

In large bowl, mix

1½ pounds ground beef
1 cup dry bread crumbs
1 cup milk
1 tablespoon Worcestershire sauce
½ teaspoon dry mustard
¼ teaspoon pepper
¼ teaspoon ground sage
1 small onion, chopped
(about ¼ cup)
1 egg

Put beef mixture in pan. Shape into an oval that looks like a football, about 8 inches long and 4½ inches wide at the middle.

Bake uncovered 55 to 60 minutes or until loaf is no longer pink in the middle.

Carefully lift meat loaf out of pan, using large pancake turners (ask an adult to help you). Put meat loaf on serving platter. Arrange pimiento slices on top to look like the lacings of a football.

TO MICROWAVE: Mix and shape as directed above except put beef mixture in rectangular microwavable dish, 10 × 6 × 1½ inches. Cover with waxed paper. (Place waxed paper on dish so it curls down instead of up. It will stay on better.)

Microwave on medium-high (70%) 10 minutes. Turn dish ½ turn. Re-cover. Microwave 10 minutes longer; turn dish ½ turn. Microwave 5 to 10 minutes longer, until center of meat loaf is no longer pink in the middle.

Leave waxed paper on meat loaf and let stand for 5 minutes. Finish as directed above.

$\mathcal{S}$teak Dinner on a Skewer

4 to 6 servings

INGREDIENTS

- Beef steak
- Italian salad dressing
- Onion
- Green bell pepper
- Cherry tomatoes

UTENSILS

- Sharp knife
- Cutting board
- Ruler
- Medium bowl
- Liquid measuring cup
- Long-handled spoon
- Plastic wrap
- 11-inch metal skewers
- Broiler pan
- Pastry brush
- Potholders

Cut into 1-inch cubes

> 1 pound beef boneless round, sirloin or chuck steak

Mix with beef in medium bowl

> ½ cup Italian salad dressing

Cover bowl with plastic wrap and refrigerate at least 1 hour but no longer than 8 hours. (For more flavor, refrigerate the longer time.)

Stir beef mixture a few times. Be sure to re-cover with plastic wrap.

Wash and cut

> 1 medium onion into 6 pieces
> 1 green bell pepper into chunks, about 1 × 1½ inches

Place the beef and vegetables on the skewers (ask an adult to help you).

Divide the beef and vegetables evenly among six 11-inch metal skewers. Leave a small space between each piece on the skewer.

End each skewer with

> 1 cherry tomato

Place skewers on rack in broiler pan. Brush the beef and vegetables with any Italian dressing remaining in the bowl.

Set oven control to broil.

Broil beef and vegetables with tops about 3 inches from heat for about 5 minutes. Ask an adult to turn over the skewers. Broil 5 minutes longer. Serve with rice if you like.

CHICKEN DINNER ON A SKEWER: Use 1 pound boneless skinless chicken breasts or thighs in place of the boneless beef steak. Marinate in Italian salad dressing no longer than 1 hour. (Marinate means letting food stand in liquid to add flavor.)

*Both **Ryan** and his family gave Steak Dinner on a Skewer the highest rating.*

*T*una and Shells Casserole

6 servings

INGREDIENTS

- Macaroni shells
- Onion
- Celery
- Pasteurized process cheese spread
- Canned tuna
- Condensed cream of chicken soup
- Milk
- Sliced pimientos
- Lemon juice

UTENSILS

- 2-quart saucepan
- Colander
- 2-quart casserole with lid
- Sharp knife
- Ruler
- Cutting board
- Dry measuring cup
- Can opener
- Long-handled spoon
- Fork
- Measuring spoons
- Potholders

Heat oven to 375°.

Prepare according to package directions, using saucepan

> 1 package (7 ounces) macaroni shells

Drain the shells in a colander. Pour shells into casserole.

Wash and chop

> 1 medium onion
> 1 stalk celery

Sprinkle shells with onion and celery.

Cut four ½-inch slices from

> 1 package (8 ounces) pasteurized process cheese spread (loaf shape)

Cut each slice into ½-inch squares until you have enough to measure 1 cup. Empty cheese squares into the casserole.

Add to the casserole and stir

> 1 can (12½ ounces) tuna, drained and flaked

Pour into the casserole

> 1 can (10¾ ounces) condensed cream of chicken soup

Fill the soup can ½ full with

> milk

Stir with fork. Pour the milk into the casserole.

Add to the casserole

> 1 jar (2 ounces) sliced pimientos, drained
> 1 teaspoon lemon juice

Stir lightly until all ingredients are mixed.

Cut thin slices from remaining cheese (enough to cover the top of the casserole). Place the slices on top of the casserole; cover.

Bake 30 minutes. Uncover and bake 5 minutes longer.

*F*ish Stick Fondue

6 servings

INGREDIENTS

- Frozen breaded fish sticks
- Dill pickle
- Mayonnaise or salad dressing
- Onion powder
- Chili sauce
- Horseradish sauce
- Lemon juice
- Worcestershire sauce

UTENSILS

- Sharp knife
- Cutting board
- Cookie sheet
- Small serving bowls
- Dry measuring cup
- Measuring spoons
- Teaspoons
- Pancake turner
- Serving platter
- Wooden picks

Heat oven to temperature given on fish stick package.

Let stand at room temperature 10 minutes

> 2 packages (8 ounces each) frozen breaded fish sticks

Cut each fish stick crosswise into 3 equal pieces. Put the fish stick pieces on cookie sheet.

Chop into small pieces and put in small bowl

> 1 large dill pickle

Stir in

> ½ cup mayonnaise or salad dressing
> ½ teaspoon onion powder

Mix in another small bowl

> ½ cup chili sauce
> 1 teaspoon horseradish sauce
> 1 teaspoon lemon juice
> ¼ teaspoon Worcestershire sauce

Bake the fish stick pieces according to package directions.

Remove fish stick pieces to serving platter, using pancake turner. Serve the fish stick pieces with the 2 bowls of dip and wooden picks for dipping.

O ven-fried Chicken

6 servings

INGREDIENTS

- Margarine or butter
- Variety baking mix
- Paprika
- Salt
- Pepper
- Chicken pieces

UTENSILS

- Rectangular pan, 13 × 9 × 2 inches
- Potholders
- Plastic bag
- Dry measuring cup
- Measuring spoons
- Tongs

Heat oven to 425°.

Heat in rectangular pan until melted (ask an adult to help you)

> 1 tablespoon margarine or butter

Remove pan from oven.

Shake in plastic bag until mixed

> ⅔ cup variety baking mix
> 1½ teaspoons paprika
> ¼ teaspoon salt
> ¼ teaspoon pepper

Shake 1 piece at a time in mixture in plastic bag

> 3 pounds chicken pieces

Tap each piece a little bit to remove any heavy layers of coating mix.

Place chicken pieces, skin sides down, in pan.

Bake uncovered for 35 minutes. Turn chicken pieces over, using tongs.

Continue baking about 15 minutes longer or until chicken is done.

TO MICROWAVE: Do not use margarine. Mix baking mix, paprika, salt and pepper and coat chicken as directed above.

Arrange chicken pieces, skin sides up and thickest parts to outside edges, in rectangular microwavable dish, 12 × 7½ × 2 inches. Cover with waxed paper. (Place waxed paper on dish so it curls down instead of up. It will stay on better.)

Microwave on high (100%) 10 minutes. Turn dish ½ turn.

Re-cover and microwave 8 to 12 minutes longer or until chicken is done.

HINT: *To make sure chicken is done, have an adult make a small cut in the chicken. If the juices run clear, it's done.*

Oven-fried Chicken, Mashed Potatoes (page 97)

*E*asy Three-Cheese Lasagne

8 servings

INGREDIENTS

- Ricotta cheese
- Parsley
- Parmesan cheese
- Dried basil
- Garlic powder
- Spaghetti sauce
- Lasagne noodles
- Shredded mozzarella cheese

UTENSILS

- Medium bowl
- Scissors
- Dry measuring cups
- Measuring spoons
- Long-handled spoon
- Rectangular bakng dish, 12 × 7½ × 2 inches
- Liquid measuring cup
- Potholders

Heat oven to 350°.

Mix together in medium bowl

> 1 container (16 ounces) ricotta cheese
> ¼ cup snipped fresh parsley or 2 tablespoons dried parsley
> 2 tablespoons grated Parmesan cheese
> 1 teaspoon dried basil
> ½ teaspoon garlic powder

Set out

> 4 cups (32 ounces) spaghetti sauce
> 8 lasagne noodles

Spread evenly over bottom of rectangular baking dish

> 1⅓ cups spaghetti sauce

Arrange over the spaghetti sauce

> 4 uncooked lasagne noodles

Spread over the noodles

> 1 cup ricotta cheese mixture
> 1 cup shredded mozzarella cheese

Spread over the mozzarella cheese

> 1⅓ cups spaghetti sauce

Make another layer with

> 4 uncooked lasagne noodles
> 1 cup ricotta cheese mixture
> 1⅓ cups spaghetti sauce

(Be sure spaghetti sauce completely covers noodles.)

Sprinkle over top

> 1 cup shredded mozzarella cheese

Bake uncovered 40 to 45 minutes or until noodles are done.

Ask an adult to remove pan from oven. It will be very hot and heavy.

Let lasagne cool 15 minutes before cutting.

*M*acaroni and Cheese

5 servings

INGREDIENTS

- Elbow macaroni
- Onion
- Margarine or butter
- Flour
- Salt
- Pepper
- Milk
- Sharp process American or Swiss cheese

UTENSILS

- 3-quart saucepan
- Dry measuring cups
- Colander
- Sharp knife
- Cutting board
- Long-handled spoon
- Measuring spoons
- Liquid measuring cup
- 1½-quart casserole
- Potholders

Heat oven to 375°.

Prepare according to package directions, using saucepan

> 1½ cups elbow macaroni

Pour into colander to drain.

Wash and chop

> 1 small onion

Cook and stir over medium heat with onion, until onion is slightly tender

> ¼ cup margarine or butter

Stir in

> ¼ cup all-purpose flour
> ½ teaspoon salt
> ¼ teaspoon pepper

Cook over low heat, stirring all the time, until mixture is smooth and bubbly.

Remove from heat.

Stir in

> 1¾ cups milk

Heat to boiling, stirring all the time. Boil and stir 1 minute. Remove from heat.

Cut into small cubes and stir into milk mixture until melted

> 8 ounces sharp process American or Swiss cheese

Place drained macaroni in casserole. Stir cheese sauce into macaroni.

Bake uncovered for 30 minutes.

Salad in a Bag

6 servings

INGREDIENTS

- Lettuce
- Tomatoes
- Radishes
- Salad dressing
- Seasoned croutons

UTENSILS

- Sharp knife
- Cutting board
- Paper towels
- Plastic bag
- Liquid measuring cup
- Large salad bowl
- Dry measuring cup

Wash and cut core from

1 medium head lettuce

Rinse lettuce under cold water. Throw away any bruised leaves.

Tear remaining lettuce into bite-size pieces. Place pieces on paper towels to dry.

Wash and cut stem ends from

2 medium tomatoes

Cut each tomato into 8 wedges.

Wash and trim

8 radishes

Cut into thin slices.

Put the lettuce pieces, tomato wedges and radish slices in plastic bag.

Pour in

⅓ cup your favorite salad dressing

Close the bag tightly with fastener or hold it closed tightly. Shake hard a few times. Empty into large salad bowl.

Sprinkle with

⅓ cup seasoned croutons

*B*uttered Carrot Nuggets

4 servings

INGREDIENTS **UTENSILS**

- Carrots
- Salt
- Margarine or butter

- Vegetable parer
- Sharp knife
- Cutting board
- Ruler
- 2-quart saucepan with lid
- Measuring spoons
- Fork
- Slotted spoon
- Serving dish

Wash and pare

6 medium carrots (about 1 pound)

Cut carrots crosswise into ½-inch pieces.

Pour 1 inch of water into saucepan.

Add carrots and

¼ teaspoon salt

Cover and heat to boiling.

Cook over medium heat 14 to 16 minutes or until carrots are tender when poked with a fork. Using slotted spoon, remove carrots to serving dish.

Stir in

1 tablespoon margarine or butter

TO MICROWAVE: Place ¼ cup water, the salt and carrots in microwavable 1-quart casserole or bowl. Cover with lid or plastic wrap. If using plastic wrap, turn back 1 edge to make a little space for steam to come out.

Microwave on high (100%) 4 minutes; stir. Replace lid and microwave 2 to 4 minutes longer or until tender.

Carefully drain. Stir in the margarine.

*B*aked Potatoes

4 servings

INGREDIENTS **UTENSILS**

- Potatoes

- Brush
- Fork
- Potholders

Heat oven to 375°.

Scrub

4 medium potatoes

Pat dry and rub with shortening for softer skins if you like. Poke with fork to allow steam to escape.

Bake potatoes 1 to 1¼ hours or until tender.

TO MICROWAVE: Choose 4 potatoes that are close to the same shape and size.

Poke potatoes with fork 2 or 3 times on top and bottom to allow steam to escape.

Arrange potatoes about 2 inches apart in a circle on microwavable paper towel in microwave oven.

Microwave potatoes uncovered on high (100%) 11 to 13 minutes or until they are soft enough to easily poke with a fork.

Let potatoes stand uncovered 5 minutes before serving.

HINT: *Serve Baked Potatoes with cheese sauce, salsa, sour cream, shredded cheese, chopped tomatoes or cooked bacon pieces.*

$\mathcal{M}$ashed Potatoes

4 servings

INGREDIENTS   UTENSILS

- Potatoes
- Milk
- Margarine or butter
- Salt
- Pepper

- Vegetable parer
- Sharp knife
- Cutting board
- 3-quart saucepan
- Potato masher
- Potholders
- Liquid measuring cup
- Measuring spoons

Wash and pare

> 2 pounds potatoes (6 medium)

Cut potatoes into large pieces.

Heat 1 inch of water to boiling in saucepan (add salt to the water if you like). Add potatoes.

Cover and heat to boiling. Turn heat down a little and boil 20 to 25 minutes.

Drain water from potatoes. Shake pan gently over low heat to dry the potatoes.

Mash potatoes until no lumps remain.

Beat in, a little at a time

> ⅓ to ½ cup milk

Add

> ¼ cup margarine or butter
> ½ teaspoon salt
> dash pepper

Beat until the potatoes are light and fluffy. Dot with additional margarine or butter and sprinkle with paprika if you like.

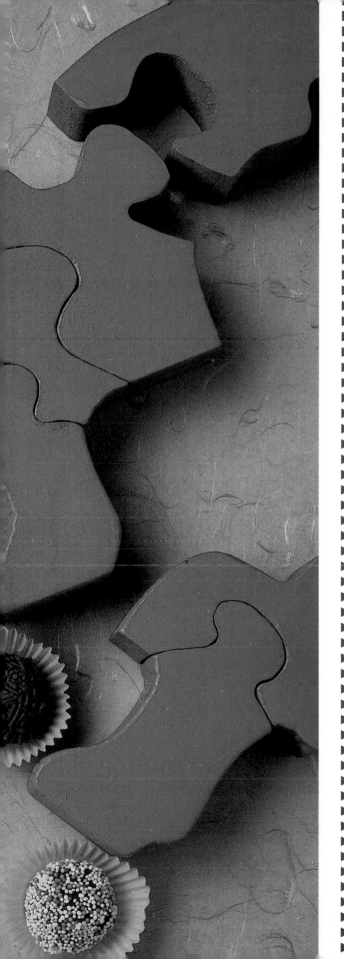

Fabulous Cookies, Cakes and More

5

Oh-So Chocolate Brownies (page 100), Chocolate Chip Cookies (page 101), Peanutty Chocolate Truffles (page 105)

Oh-So-Chocolate Brownies

36 brownies

INGREDIENTS

- Shortening
- Unsweetened chocolate
- Granulated sugar
- Eggs
- Vanilla
- Flour
- Chopped nuts
- Baking powder
- Salt
- Powdered sugar

UTENSILS

- Rectangular pan, 13 × 9 × 2 inches
- 2-quart saucepan
- Dry measuring cups
- Measuring spoons
- Long-handled spoon
- Rubber scraper
- Potholders
- Wire cooling rack
- Table knife
- Ruler

Heat oven to 350°.

Grease rectangular pan with shortening.

Heat in saucepan over low heat until melted

> 4 squares (1 ounce each) unsweetened chocolate
> ⅔ cup shortening

Remove from heat. Stir in

> 2 cups granulated sugar
> 4 eggs
> 1 teaspoon vanilla

Stir in

> 1¼ cups all-purpose flour
> 1 cup chopped nuts
> 1 teaspoon baking powder
> ½ teaspoon salt

Spread the batter in pan with rubber scraper.

Bake 30 minutes or until brownies start to pull away from sides of pan. Do not overbake!

Cool the brownies slightly on wire rack. Cut into 2 × 1½-inch bars. Cool completely.

Sprinkle with

> powdered sugar

$\mathcal{C}$hocolate Chip Cookies

24 cookies

INGREDIENTS

- Granulated sugar
- Brown sugar
- Margarine or butter
- Egg
- Flour
- Baking soda
- Salt
- Semisweet chocolate chips
- Chopped nuts

UTENSILS

- Large bowl
- Dry measuring cups
- Long-handled spoon
- Measuring spoons
- Tablespoon
- Cookie sheet
- Ruler
- Potholders
- Pancake turner
- Wire cooling rack

Heat oven to 375°.

Mix in large bowl with spoon

> ½ cup granulated sugar
> ½ cup packed brown sugar
> ½ cup margarine or butter, softened
> 1 egg

Stir in

> 1½ cups all-purpose flour
> ½ teaspoon baking soda
> ½ teaspoon salt

Stir in

> 1 cup semisweet chocolate chips
> ½ cup chopped nuts

Drop dough by rounded tablespoonfuls about 2 inches apart onto cookie sheet.

Bake 10 to 12 minutes or until light brown.

Let cookies cool slightly. Remove from cookie sheet to wire rack, using pancake turner.

HINT: *You can use 1 cup of candy-coated chocolate candies instead of the semisweet chocolate chips.*

I ♥ Shortbread

About 16 cookies

INGREDIENTS

- Butter*
- Sugar
- Flour
- Salt
- Powdered sugar

UTENSILS

- Medium bowl
- Dry measuring cups
- Long-handled spoon
- Rolling pin
- Heart-shaped or your favorite shape cookie cutter
- Cookie sheet
- Potholders
- Pancake turner
- Wire cooling rack
- Small sieve

Heat oven to 350°.

Mix together in medium bowl

> ¾ cup butter, softened
> ¼ cup sugar

Stir in

> 1¾ cups all-purpose flour
> dash of salt

▶ Mixture will be dry and crumbly. Pinch mixture together with clean hands until it all sticks together. Shape dough into a ball.

▶ Sprinkle a clean surface (such as a kitchen counter or breadboard) with flour.

▶ Place dough on surface. Roll or pat out dough ¼ inch thick. Cut dough with 2-inch heart-shaped cookie cutter, or use your favorite shape cookie cutter.

▶ Place hearts about ½ inch apart on cookie sheet.

▶ Bake about 10 to 15 minutes or until very light golden brown on the edges.

▶ Take the cookies off the cookie sheet right away with pancake turner.

▶ Cool shortbread on wire rack.

▶ Put in sieve and shake over each cookie to cover lightly

> powdered sugar

＊Margarine is not recommended.

*F*antastic Fudge

64 pieces

INGREDIENTS	UTENSILS
■ Margarine or butter	■ Square pan, 8 × 8 × 2 inches
■ Semisweet chocolate chips	■ 2-quart saucepan
■ Sweetened condensed milk	■ Long-handled spoon
■ Vanilla	■ Can opener
■ Salt	■ Measuring spoons
	■ Table knife
	■ Ruler

Grease square pan with margarine or butter.

Put in saucepan

> 1 package (12 ounces) and
> 1 package (6 ounces) semisweet
> chocolate chips

Heat chocolate chips over low heat, stirring a few times, until melted. Remove saucepan from heat.

Stir into melted chocolate

> 1 can (14 ounces) sweetened
> condensed milk
> 1 teaspoon vanilla
> dash of salt

Pour fudge into pan. Spread fudge evenly in pan with back of spoon. Refrigerate 2 hours or until firm.

Cut fudge into 1-inch squares.

FANTASTIC NUTTY FUDGE: Stir ½ to ¾ cup chopped nuts into melted chocolate.

TO MICROWAVE: Put chocolate chips in 1½-quart microwavable casserole or bowl. Cover with lid or plastic wrap. If using plastic wrap, turn back 1 edge to make a space for steam to come out.

Microwave on medium (50%) 5 to 7 minutes or until chips are shiny. Stir until smooth. Finish as directed above.

*P*eanutty Chocolate Truffles

About 20 truffles

INGREDIENTS

- Semisweet chocolate chips
- Peanut butter
- Milk
- Margarine or butter
- Salt
- Candy decorations

UTENSILS

- Cookie sheets or dinner plates
- Waxed paper
- 2-quart saucepan
- Dry measuring cup
- Measuring spoons
- Long-handled spoon
- Medium bowl
- Rubber scraper
- Teaspoon

Line cookie sheets or 2 dinner plates with waxed paper.

Mix together in saucepan

> 1 package (6 ounces) semisweet chocolate chips
> ½ cup peanut butter
> 2 tablespoons milk
> 2 tablespoons margarine or butter
> dash of salt

Heat mixture over medium heat, stirring all the time, until the chocolate is melted and the mixture is smooth.

Pour mixture into medium bowl. (Be sure to clean the saucepan well with a rubber scraper to get all the chocolate mixture.)

Cover and refrigerate at least 1½ hours or until chocolate mixture is firm.

Shape heaping teaspoonfuls of the chocolate mixture into balls.

Gently roll each ball in

> candy decorations (such as multicolored or chocolate-flavored shot)

Place the truffles on the cookie sheets. Refrigerate at least 1 hour or until firm.

Cover and refrigerate any remaining truffles.

TO MICROWAVE: Put all ingredients except candy decorations in 1½-quart microwavable casserole. Cover with lid or plastic wrap. If using plastic wrap, turn back 1 edge to make a little space for steam to come out.

Microwave on medium (50%) 3 to 4 minutes or until chocolate has softened and mixture can be stirred smooth.

Finish as directed above.

Milk Chocolate Brownie Cake

16 servings

INGREDIENTS

- Shortening
- Margarine or butter
- Cocoa
- Flour
- Sugar
- Baking soda
- Salt
- Eggs
- Plain yogurt or sour cream
- Cherry Frosting (page 108)

UTENSILS

- Jelly roll pan, 15½ × 10½ × 1 inch
- 2½-quart saucepan
- Liquid measuring cup
- Dry measuring cups
- Long-handled spoon
- Measuring spoons
- Wooden picks
- Potholders
- Wire cooling rack
- Table knife

Heat oven to 375°.

Grease jelly roll pan with shortening.

Heat in saucepan, stirring a few times

> 1 cup margarine or butter
> 1 cup water
> ⅓ cup cocoa

▶ Remove from heat.

▶ Stir in

> 2 cups all-purpose flour
> 2 cups sugar
> 1 teaspoon baking soda
> ½ teaspoon salt
> 2 eggs
> ½ cup plain yogurt or sour cream

Pour batter into the pan. (Batter will be very thin.)

Bake 20 to 25 minutes or until wooden pick inserted in center of cake comes out clean. Cool on wire rack.

Follow directions on page 108 to make

> Cherry Frosting

Frost cake when cool.

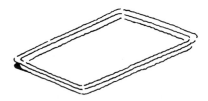

Milk Chocolate Brownie Cake

*C*herry Frosting

About 2½ cups frosting

INGREDIENTS

- Maraschino cherries
- Margarine or butter
- Cocoa
- Milk
- Powdered sugar
- Almond extract
- Salt

UTENSILS

- Scissors
- Paper towels
- 3-quart saucepan
- Dry measuring cup
- Liquid measuring cup
- Long-handled spoon
- Measuring spoons

Cut each into 6 pieces with scissors

> 1 jar (4 ounces) maraschino cherries, drained

Place cherry pieces on paper towels to dry.

In saucepan heat to boiling, stirring a few times

> ½ cup margarine or butter
> ⅓ cup cocoa
> ⅓ cup milk

Remove from heat.

Gradually add and beat until smooth

> 1 package (16 ounces) powdered sugar

Stir in cherry pieces and

> 1 teaspoon almond extract
> dash of salt

*A*ngel Food Cake with Snowstorm Frosting

16 servings

INGREDIENTS

- Angel food or chiffon cake
- Frozen whipped topping, thawed
- Flaked coconut

UTENSILS

- Serving plate
- Table knife
- Dry measuring cups

Put on serving plate

> 1 angel food or chiffon cake

Frost the cake with

> 1 container (4 ounces) frozen whipped topping, thawed

Sprinkle with

> 2⅔ cups flaked coconut

Refrigerate until serving time.

HINT: *Tinted coconut can be substituted for plain coconut. Shake coconut with 4 or 5 drops food color in tightly covered container until coconut is evenly tinted.*

*H*ot Fudge Pudding Cake

9 servings

INGREDIENTS

- Flour
- Sugar
- Cocoa
- Baking powder
- Salt
- Milk
- Peanut butter
- Vegetable oil
- Vanilla
- Brown sugar

UTENSILS

- Large bowl
- Dry measuring cups
- Measuring spoons
- Long-handled spoon
- Liquid measuring cup
- Square pan, 9 × 9 × 2 inches
- Rubber scraper
- Small bowl
- Potholders
- Dessert dishes

Heat oven to 350°.

Mix in large bowl

> 1 cup all-purpose flour
> ¾ cup sugar
> 2 tablespoons cocoa
> 2 teaspoons baking powder
> ¼ teaspoon salt

▶ Stir in until mixture is smooth

> ½ cup milk
> ½ cup peanut butter
> 2 tablespoons vegetable oil
> 1 teaspoon vanilla

Spoon mixture into square pan. Spread evenly to edges of pan.

Stir together in small bowl until well blended

> 1 cup packed brown sugar
> ¼ cup cocoa

Sprinkle brown sugar–cocoa mixture over batter.

Pour over brown sugar mixture but do not stir

> 1¾ cups hot water

Bake 45 minutes.

To serve, spoon each serving upside down into dessert dishes. Spoon any extra sauce over the top. (Sauce will thicken as it stands.) Best served warm.

*U*pside-down Pineapple Cake

9 servings

INGREDIENTS

- Margarine or butter
- Brown sugar
- Canned sliced pineapple
- Maraschino cherries
- Flour
- Granulated sugar
- Shortening
- Milk
- Baking powder
- Salt
- Egg

UTENSILS

- 10-inch ovenproof skillet or square pan, 9 × 9 × 2 inches
- Potholders
- Dry measuring cups
- Can opener
- Large bowl
- Electric mixer
- Rubber scraper
- Liquid measuring cup
- Measuring spoons
- Wooden picks
- Heatproof serving plate

Heat oven to 350°.

Heat in ovenproof skillet or square pan in oven until melted

> ¼ cup margarine or butter

Sprinkle over margarine

> ⅔ cup packed brown sugar

Arrange on top

> 1 can (about 16 ounces) sliced pineapple, drained

Place in center of each pineapple slice

> 1 maraschino cherry

Beat in large bowl with electric mixer on low speed 30 seconds, scraping with rubber scraper all the time

> 1⅓ cups all-purpose flour
> 1 cup granulated sugar
> ⅓ cup shortening
> ¾ cup milk
> 1½ teaspoons baking powder
> ½ teaspoon salt
> 1 egg

Beat on high speed 3 minutes, scraping bowl a few times. Pour over fruit in skillet.

Bake 45 to 50 minutes for skillet, 55 to 60 minutes for pan, or until wooden pick inserted in center comes out clean.

Turn skillet upside down on heatproof serving plate right away.

Let skillet remain over cake a few minutes. Serve warm, and if you like, with sweetened whipped cream.

trawberry Shortcakes

6 servings

INGREDIENTS

- Strawberries
- Sugar
- Variety baking mix
- Half-and-half
- Margarine or butter
- Sweetened whipped cream

UTENSILS

- Colander
- Medium bowl
- Wooden spoon
- Small sharp knife
- Cutting board
- Dry measuring cups
- Large bowl
- Liquid measuring cup
- Measuring spoons
- Rolling pin
- 3-inch round cutter
- Cookie sheet
- Potholders
- Table knife
- Spoon

Rinse in colander

> 1 quart strawberries

Let them dry or gently pat dry with a clean towel.

Remove stems. Cut strawberries in half and mix in medium bowl with

> ½ cup sugar

Heat oven to 425°.

Mix in large bowl until soft dough forms

> 2⅓ cups variety baking mix
> ½ cup half-and-half
> 3 tablespoons sugar
> 3 tablespoons margarine or butter, melted

Sprinkle a clean surface (such as a kitchen counter or breadboard) with baking mix or flour. Place dough on surface and gently smooth it into a ball. Knead dough 8 to 10 times.

Roll dough ½ inch thick. Cut with floured round cutter to make 6 shortcakes.

Carefully place shortcakes about 1 inch apart on cookie sheet.

Bake 12 to 15 minutes or until golden brown.

Split shortcakes in half horizontally using knife. Spoon strawberries between halves and over tops. Top with sweetened whipped cream.

*F*rozen Chocolate Crunch

4 servings

INGREDIENTS

- Whipping cream
- Chocolate sauce
- Almond brickle chips
- Vanilla

UTENSILS

- Medium bowl
- Eggbeater
- Liquid measuring cup
- Measuring spoons
- Rubber scraper
- Small dessert bowls or custard cups

Chill medium bowl in freezer about 15 minutes or until cold.

Beat in chilled bowl with eggbeater until stiff

1 cup whipping cream

Carefully fold into whipped cream with rubber scraper

⅓ cup chocolate sauce 2 tablespoons almond brickle chips 1 teaspoon vanilla

Divide mixture equally among 4 small dessert bowls or custard cups.

Freeze about 2 hours or until firm.

HINT: *If Frozen Chocolate Crunch freezes too hard, just set it out at room temperature about 5 minutes to soften a little before serving.*

*F*udge Sundae Pie

8 to 10 servings

INGREDIENTS

- 7-inch chocolate-flavored pie crust
- Ice cream or frozen yogurt
- Fudge sauce

UTENSILS

- Rubber scraper
- Ice-cream scoop
- Dry measuring cup

Spread in the pie crust with rubber scraper

1 quart of your favorite ice cream or frozen yogurt, softened

Freeze about 1 hour or until ice cream is firm.

Spread evenly over the ice cream

¾ cup fudge sauce

Freeze about 1 hour or until the sauce is set.

*We enjoyed **Malia**'s reaction to Fudge Sundae Pie, "IT WAS SOOOOOO GOOD!"*

Caramel Apples

6 apples

INGREDIENTS

- Apples
- Granola, chopped peanuts or chopped candy-coated chocolate candies
- Vanilla caramels
- Peanut butter
- Ground cinnamon

UTENSILS

- Wooden sticks
- Waxed paper
- Measuring spoons
- 1½-quart saucepan
- Dry measuring cup
- Long-handled spoon

Wash

> 6 medium apples

Poke a wooden stick in the stem end of each apple.

Using 1 tablespoon of granola for each mound, make 6 mounds about 3 inches apart on waxed paper, using

> 6 tablespoons granola, chopped peanuts or chopped candy-coated chocolate candies

Heat in saucepan over low heat about 20 minutes or until caramels are melted and mixture is smooth

> 1 package (14 ounces) vanilla caramels
> 3 tablespoons water
> ¼ cup creamy peanut butter
> ½ teaspoon ground cinnamon

Remove from heat. Dip each apple in the hot caramel mixture and spoon mixture over the apple until it is completely coated.

Hold the apple right side up by the stick for a second, then place it stick side up on one of the mounds of granola. Turn the apple so all the granola sticks to it.

Refrigerate about 1 hour or until the caramel coating is firm.

CHOCOLATY CARAMEL APPLES: Use only 2 tablespoons of water. Use ¼ cup chocolate chips in place of the peanut butter and chocolate caramels in place of the vanilla caramels.

TO MICROWAVE: Prepare apples and granola as directed above except use only 2 tablespoons of water. Put water, caramels, peanut butter and ground cinnamon in 4-cup microwavable measure.

Microwave uncovered on high (100%) 2 minutes; stir.

Microwave 30 to 60 seconds longer or until caramels can be stirred smooth. Finish as directed above. (If caramel thickens, microwave uncovered on high 30 seconds.)

Following pages: Caramel Apples

*C*hocolate-dipped Strawberries

4 to 6 servings

INGREDIENTS

- Strawberries
- Semisweet chocolate chips
- Shortening

UTENSILS

- Cookie sheet or dinner plates
- Waxed paper
- Colander
- 1-quart saucepan
- Long-handled spoon
- Fork

Line cookie sheet or 2 dinner plates with waxed paper.

Rinse in colander

1 pint strawberries

Let strawberries dry or gently pat them dry with a clean towel. Remove the stems if you like.

Put in saucepan

1 package (6 ounces) semisweet chocolate chips ½ teaspoon shortening

Heat chocolate chips over low heat, stirring a few times, until melted. Remove saucepan from heat.

For each strawberry, poke the stem end with fork and dip it into the melted chocolate. (Do not cover all of the strawberry with chocolate.) Place strawberries on cookie sheet. Refrigerate uncovered about 30 minutes or until chocolate is firm.

TO MICROWAVE: Prepare as directed above except put chocolate chips and shortening in 1-quart microwavable casserole or bowl. Cover with lid or plastic wrap. If using plastic wrap, turn back 1 edge to make a little space for steam to come out. Microwave on medium (50%) 3 to 5 minutes or until chips are shiny. Stir until smooth. Finish as directed above.

HINT: *Chocolate-dipped Strawberries can be stored in the refrigerator up to 24 hours.*

Chocolate-dipped Strawberries

For That Special Occasion

6

Heart Cake (page 128)

Easy Party Pot Roast

8 servings

INGREDIENTS

- Beef pot roast
- Garlic powder
- Pepper
- Condensed French onion soup
- Canned stewed tomatoes

UTENSILS

- Dutch oven
- Measuring spoons
- Can opener
- Potholders
- Long-handled fork
- Serving platter
- Long-handled spoon

Heat oven to 350°.

Put in Dutch oven

> 4-pound beef arm, blade or cross-rib pot roast

Sprinkle over pot roast

> ½ teaspoon garlic powder
> ⅛ teaspoon pepper

Pour over roast

> 1 can (10½ ounces) condensed French onion soup
> 1 can (14½ ounces) stewed tomatoes

Cover and cook roast about 3 hours or until roast is tender when poked with fork. (Be sure to have an adult uncover the roast and poke it with the fork. It will be VERY hot.)

When roast is done, ask an adult to put it on a serving platter. Spoon some of the pan juices over it.

*Easy Party Pot Roast lives up to its name! "It's easy to make," says **Malia**.*

Baked Cheese with Apples

4 to 6 servings

INGREDIENTS

- Brie or Camembert cheese
- Chopped nuts
- Apples

UTENSILS

- Small baking dish
- Measuring spoons
- Potholders
- Apple corer
- Sharp knife
- Cutting board
- Table knife

Heat oven to 350°.

Put in small baking dish

> 1 round (4½ ounces) Brie or Camembert cheese

Top cheese with

> 2 tablespoons chopped nuts

Bake 10 to 15 minutes or until cheese is warm and soft.

While cheese is baking, wash, core and cut into thin wedges

2 medium apples

Serve with a table knife to spread cheese on apples.

TO MICROWAVE: Prepare cheese as directed above except put it in a microwavable dish.

Microwave uncovered on medium (50%) 45 seconds to 1½ minutes or until cheese is warm and soft.

Jennifer *decided to make Baked Cheese with Apples with pecans. She also suggested serving it with crackers. Both are delicious ideas!*

*S*pecial Quiche

6 servings

INGREDIENTS

- 9-inch frozen pie crust shell, thawed
- Shredded Swiss or Gruyère cheese
- Canned sliced mushrooms
- Eggs
- Half-and-half
- Salt
- Pepper

UTENSILS

- Dry measuring cup
- Can opener
- Medium bowl
- Liquid measuring cup
- Measuring spoons
- Eggbeater or wire whisk
- Potholders
- Table knife

Heat oven to 400°.

Sprinkle in pie crust shell

1 cup shredded Swiss or Gruyère cheese (4 ounces)
1 can (3 ounces) sliced mushrooms, drained

Mix together in medium bowl with eggbeater or wire whisk

2 eggs
1 cup half-and-half
¼ teaspoon salt
dash of pepper

Pour egg mixture over cheese and mushrooms in pie crust shell. Ask an adult to help put the unbaked quiche in the oven. (The pie shell will be very full and easy to spill.)

Bake about 30 minutes or until the quiche is golden brown and a knife inserted in the center comes out clean.

Let quiche cool about 10 minutes before cutting it.

Festive Garlic Bread

1 loaf

INGREDIENTS

- Margarine or butter
- Parsley
- Garlic powder
- 1-pound loaf French bread

UTENSILS

- Small bowl
- Measuring spoons
- Spoon
- Sharp knife
- Cutting board
- Ruler
- Table knife
- Aluminum foil
- Potholders

Heat oven to 400°.

Mix together in small bowl

> ½ cup margarine or butter, softened
> 1 tablespoon snipped fresh or
> 1 teaspoon dried parsley
> ¼ to ½ teaspoon garlic powder

Cut into 1-inch slices, but DO NOT cut through the bottom of

> 1-pound loaf French bread

Spread the margarine mixture between all the slices. Wrap bread in aluminum foil.

Bake about 15 minutes or until the bread is hot. To serve, let each person pull off a slice of bread.

Chunky Corn Bread

12 servings

INGREDIENTS

- Shortening
- Cornmeal
- Flour
- Milk
- Vegetable oil
- Sugar
- Baking powder
- Salt
- Eggs
- Canned corn

UTENSILS

- Square pan, 8 × 8 × 2 inches
- Large bowl
- Dry measuring cups
- Liquid measuring cup
- Measuring spoons
- Long-handled spoon
- Can opener
- Wooden picks
- Potholders

Heat oven to 400°.

Grease square pan with shortening.

Beat together in large bowl until smooth

> 1 cup cornmeal
> 1 cup all-purpose flour
> 1 cup milk
> ¼ cup vegetable oil
> 1 tablespoon sugar
> 2 teaspoons baking powder
> 1 teaspoon salt
> 2 eggs

Stir in

> ½ cup canned corn

Pour mixture into the pan.

Bake about 25 minutes or until golden brown and wooden pick inserted in center comes out clean. Serve warm.

HINT: *Refrigerate any leftover corn in a covered container to use at another time.*

*G*olden Oven Fries

6 servings

INGREDIENTS

- Potatoes
- Vegetable oil

UTENSILS

- Jelly roll pan, 15½ × 10½ × 1 inch
- Sharp knife
- Cutting board
- Ruler
- Measuring spoons
- Pancake turner
- Potholders

Heat oven to 450°.

Coat inside of jelly roll pan with vegetable oil.

Wash and pat dry

3 large baking potatoes (about 8 ounces each)

Cut each potato into ½-inch slices. Cut the slices into ½-inch strips.

Place potatoes in jelly roll pan.

Drizzle potatoes with

3 to 4 tablespoons vegetable oil

With clean hands, carefully toss the potatoes to coat them evenly with oil.

Bake potatoes about 40 minutes or until golden brown. Ask an adult to turn the potatoes a few times with a pancake turner while they are cooking.

When potatoes are done, sprinkle with salt if you like.

*E*aster Hat Cake

12 servings

INGREDIENTS

- Shortening
- Flour
- Yellow or lemon cake mix with pudding
- Fluffy white frosting mix

UTENSILS

- Round pan, 9 × 1½ inches
- Round pan, 8 × 1½ inches
- Potholders
- Wire cooling rack
- Scissors
- Paper
- Ruler
- Small knife
- Small bowl
- Long spatula
- Ribbon
- Flowers

Grease both round pans with shortening. Place a small amount of flour in each pan. Shake to coat pans; empty out excess flour.

Prepare according to package directions

> 1 package (18¼ ounces) yellow or lemon cake mix with pudding

Pour half the batter into each pan. (The 9-inch layer will be for the brim of the hat, the 8-inch for the crown).

Bake according to package directions.

Cool layers completely. Remove cakes from pans.

Cut 6-inch circle of paper. Set on the 8-inch layer. Cut around it with a small knife to make a 6-inch round layer; set on top of 9-inch layer.

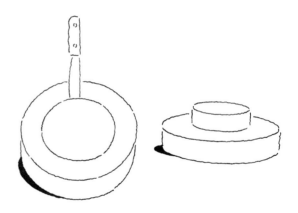

Prepare according to package directions

> 1 package (7.2 ounces) fluffy white frosting mix

Frost the cake. Trim hat with ribbon and tiny flowers.

HINT: *Use leftover cake for snacking. Enjoy it plain or top with fresh fruit.*

*H*eart Cake

12 servings

INGREDIENTS

- Shortening
- Flour
- White or sour cream white cake mix with pudding
- Fluffy white frosting mix
- Red food color

UTENSILS

- Round pan, 8 × 1½ inches
- Square pan, 8 × 8 × 2 inches
- Potholders
- Wire cooling rack
- Large tray
- Sharp knife
- Long spatula

Grease round pan and square pan with shortening. Place a small amount of flour in each pan. Shake to coat pans; empty out excess flour.

Prepare according to package directions

> 1 package (18¼ ounces) white or sour cream white cake mix with pudding

Divide batter between pans.

Bake according to package directions.

Cool layers completely. Remove cakes from pans.

Set square cake on large tray with one point toward you. Cut round layer in half. Arrange each half with cut side against top corners of square cake to form a heart.

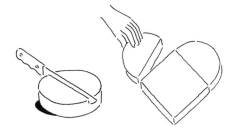

Prepare according to package directions

> 1 package (7.2 ounces) fluffy white frosting mix

Add to frosting to tint pink

> few drops of red food color

Frost cake. Be sure to cover top of cake well, especially over the cut sections.

Decorate as you like.

Jack-O'-Lantern Cake

12 servings

INGREDIENTS

- Shortening
- Flour
- Spice or carrot cake mix with pudding
- Creamy Frosting (right)
- Red food color
- Yellow food color
- Flat black jelly candies
- Candy corn

UTENSILS

- Round pans, 9 × 1½ inches or 8 × 1½ inches
- Potholders
- Wire cooling rack
- Long spatula

Grease 2 round pans with shortening. Place a small amount of flour in each pan. Shake to coat pans; empty out excess flour.

Prepare according to package directions

1 package (18¼ ounces) spice or carrot cake mix with pudding

Pour half of batter into each pan. Bake according to directions on package. Cool layers completely. Remove cakes from pans.

Follow the directions on the right to prepare

Creamy Frosting

Tint Creamy Frosting by using a few drops of red and yellow food color. Start slow, adding more drops to get the color of orange you like.

Fill the layers and frost cake.

Make a jack-o'-lantern face with

flat black jelly candies candy corn

Creamy Frosting

About 2 cups frosting

INGREDIENTS

- Powdered sugar
- Margarine or butter
- Milk
- Vanilla

UTENSILS

- Medium bowl
- Dry measuring cups
- Long-handled spoon
- Measuring spoons

Mix in medium bowl

3 cups powdered sugar ⅓ cup margarine or butter, softened

Stir in

2 tablespoons milk 1½ teaspoons vanilla

Beat frosting until smooth and of spreading consistency. If frosting is too thick, add a little more milk. If frosting is too thin, add a little more powdered sugar.

*E*asy Penuche Frosting

About 2½ cups frosting

INGREDIENTS

- Margarine or butter
- Brown sugar
- Milk
- Powdered sugar

UTENSILS

- Square pan, 8 × 8 × 2 inches
- 2-quart saucepan
- Dry measuring cup
- Long-handled spoon
- Liquid measuring cup

Fill square pan about ⅓ of the way to the top with cold water and ice cubes.

Heat in saucepan over low heat until melted

½ cup margarine or butter

Stir in

1 cup packed brown sugar

Cook over low heat 2 minutes, stirring a few times.

Stir in

¼ cup milk

Heat to rolling boil, stirring all the time. Remove from heat and set the saucepan in the pan of cold water and ice.

When the mixture has cooled so that you can comfortably hold your hand on the bottom of the saucepan, gradually stir in

2 cups powdered sugar

Put the saucepan back in the pan of ice water and beat the sugar mixture until it becomes thick enough to spread. If the frosting is too thin, add a little more powdered sugar. If it is too thick, add a few drops of hot water.

Big Burger Cake (page 132)

*B*ig Burger Cake

12 servings

INGREDIENTS

- Shortening
- Flour
- Golden pound cake mix
- Sesame seed
- Easy Penuche Frosting (page 130)
- Cocoa
- Strawberry preserves

UTENSILS

- 1½-quart casserole
- Wooden picks
- Wire cooling rack
- Serving plate
- Cookie sheet
- Measuring spoons
- Ruler
- Long serrated knife
- Dry measuring cup
- Long spatula
- Small bowl
- Spoon

Heat oven to 300°.

Grease casserole with shortening. Sprinkle a little flour into the casserole and shake gently from side to side until the flour coats the bottom and side. Empty out excess flour.

Prepare according to package directions

> 1 package (16 ounces) golden pound cake mix

Pour batter into casserole.

Bake 1 hour 5 minutes to 1 hour 10 minutes or until wooden pick inserted in center comes out clean. Cool cake on wire rack 10 minutes. Remove from casserole and place rounded side up on serving plate.

While the cake is cooling, sprinkle on cookie sheet

> 1 tablespoon sesame seed

Bake about 5 minutes or until golden.

Follow the directions on page 130 to prepare

> Easy Penuche Frosting

The cake will be easier to cut if you mark it with wooden picks to guide the knife. Insert 1 row of wooden picks (about 2 inches apart) 1 inch from the bottom of the cake and another row 2 inches from the bottom. Use the wooden picks as a guide to cut the cake into 3 layers of equal thickness: 1 layer for the top bun, 1 layer for the hamburger and 1 layer for the bottom bun.

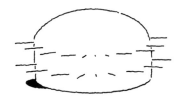

Frost the bottom layer with about ⅓ cup frosting.

Measure ⅓ cup of the remaining frosting into small bowl and stir in

2 tablespoons cocoa

If the frosting seems stiff, stir in ½ teaspoon water. Place the middle (hamburger) layer on top of the bottom layer. Frost the middle layer with the cocoa-flavored frosting.

Place the top (rounded) layer on top of the middle layer. Frost with remaining frosting.

Drizzle side of middle layer with

2 tablespoons strawberry preserves (to resemble ketchup)

Sprinkle top of the cake with the toasted sesame seed.

Cranberry-Apple Sparkler

1 serving

INGREDIENTS   UTENSILS

- Cranberry-apple juice
- Sparkling water
- Orange slice

- Tall glass

Fill tall glass ⅔ full with ice cubes.

Pour in enough to just cover ice cubes

cranberry-apple juice

Fill glass with

sparkling water

Decorate glass with an orange slice over the rim.

Hilary *added a sparkle for her tastebuds with Cranberry-Apple Sparkler. She enjoyed tasting this recipe because "it was fun to try a new drink."*

Following Pages: Fiesta Chili (page 82), Jack-O'-Lantern Cake (page 129)

Menus

DINNER FOR SOMEONE SPECIAL

Steak Dinner on a Skewer (page 87)
Rice
Sliced Tomatoes with Italian Dressing
Fudge Sundae Pie (page 114)

WINTER HOLIDAY PARTY

Hot Apple Cider
Zippy Vegetable Dip (page 19) and
Vegetable "Dippers"
Toasty Hot Dog Roll-ups (page 64)
Baked Cheese with Apples
(pages 122–123)
Assorted Cookies

VALENTINE'S DAY

Cranberry Juice
Quick Cheeseburger Pie (page 83)
Fruit Gelatin
Heart Cake (page 128)

SLUMBER PARTY

Hungry-time Hoagies (page 63)
Celery and Carrot Sticks
Golden Oven Fries (page 125)
Big Burger Cake (pages 132–133)

BACKYARD PICNIC

Oven-fried Chicken (page 90)
Crunchy Tortellini Salad (page 71)
Festive Garlic Bread (page 124)
Lemonade
Oh-So-Chocolate Brownies (page 100)

BREAKFAST IN BED FOR MOM

Orange Juice
Croissants or Toast with Strawberry
Jam
Special Quiche (page 123)
Sausage Links

HALLOWEEN PARTY

Orange Soda
Roasted Pumpkin Seeds
Fiesta Chili (page 82)
Chunky Corn Bread (page 124)
Jack-O'-Lantern Cake (page 129)

BIRTHDAY PARTY FOR DAD

Easy Party Pot Roast (page 122)
Baked Potatoes (pages 96–97)
Salad in a Bag (page 95)
Cake and Ice Cream

Index